THE TRAIL OF THE TRAMP

BY

A-No. 1 (AKA Leon Ray Livingston)

THE FAMOUS TRAMP

WRITTEN BY HIMSELF

FROM ACTUAL EXPERIENCES

OF HIS OWN LIFE.

Illustrated by

JOSEPH EARL SHROCK

EIGHTH EDITION

Yours truly
G.H.NOL1K
The Rambler

An Introductory.
CHAPTER I.
"The Harvester."

"It is my turn tonight to relate for your entertainment a story of my past, and I shall repeat to you the most pathetic happening that I have ever experienced in all my life. I have never been able to eradicate its details from my memory, as I witnessed its beginning with my own eyes, and its ending, many years later, was told to me by one of the principal participants."

This Evening It Was Canada Joe's Turn to Tell a Story.

"I shall not repeat to you one of the same, old, time-worn tales of how slick hoboes beat trains, nor fabled romance concerning harmless wanderlusters, nor jokes at the expense of the poor but honest man in search of legitimate employment, but I shall relate to you a rarely strange story that will stir your hearts to their innermost depths and will cause you to shudder at the villainy of certain human beings, who, like vultures seeking carrion, hunt for other people's sons with the intention of turning them into tramps, beggars, drunkards and criminals —into despised outcasts."

The man who spoke was a typical old-time harvester, who was known amongst his acquaintances as "Canada Joe", and the men for whose entertainment he offered to tell this story had, like himself, worked from dawn until nearly dark in the blazing sun and the choking dust of the harvest field, gathering the bounteous wheat crop of one of South Dakota's "Bonanza" farms, and who, now that their day's toil had been accomplished and their suppers partaken of, were lounging upon the velvety lawn in front of the ranch foreman's residence, and while the silvery stars were peacefully twinkling in the heavens overhead, they were repeating stories of their checkered lives, which only too often brought back memories of those long-ago days, before they too had joined the flotsam of that class of the "underworld", who, too proud to degrade themselves to the level of outright vagrancy while yet there was a chance to exchange long and weary hours of the hardest kind of labor for the right to earn an honorable existence, were nevertheless, included by critical society in that large clan of homeless drifters—"The Tramps".

And this evening it was for "Canada Joe" to tell a story.

CHAPTER II.
"The Samaritans."

Many years have passed since the day that "Peoria Red" and I were caught out of doors and entirely unprepared to face one of the worst blizzards that ever swept down from the Arctic regions across the shelterless plains of the Dakotas.

We had been "hoboing" a ride upon a freight train and had been fired off by its crew at a lone siding about fifty miles east of Minot, North Dakota. In those early days trains were few and the chances that one of them would stop at this lone siding were so small that we decided to walk to the nearest water tank, which in those days of small engines were never more than twenty miles apart, and there catch another ride.

It was a clear winter morning, and the sun's rays were vacillating upon the snow, that like a gigantic bedspread covered the landscape, and which made walking upon the hidden and uneven track a most wearisome task, the more so as neither of us had tasted a mouthful of food since the preceding day's dinner hour. While we were debating and wondering how and where we would rake up a meal amongst the few and widely scattered ranches, the wind veered to the north and commenced to blow with ever increasing force. Soon heavy, gray clouds followed in its wake, and quickly overcast the sky, and by two o'clock in the afternoon the rapidly growing fury of the wind commenced to drive sharp pointed particles of snow before it, which, as the storm increased to cyclonic proportions, changed to masses of rotating darts, which cut into the exposed portions of our illy-clad bodies and made breathing a serious problem.

We soon gave up the small hope of being able to reach a ranch house, as to leave the railroad track would have spelled death, as we would have lost our way in a few minutes, as even now, while it was yet broad daylight, we could barely see a couple of telegraph poles ahead of us, and when night approached the ever increasing fury of the blizzard greatly reduced even this short distance.

Staggering against the snow storm our one ardent prayer was that we would reach our only hope for succor—one of those railroad section houses, which are located ten miles apart along the right of way of every railroad, and are the homes of a foreman and a crew of laborers who repair and keep the track under constant surveillance.

Every moment the cold increased, and although we were spurred on to almost superhuman efforts by sheer desperation to thwart the fate we knew would be ours should we falter by the way, gradually our strength failed us, and although we tried to encourage each other to quicker progress, it took every vestige of our will power to drag our benumbed feet from step to step against the howling, snow-laden hurricane.

Peoria Red piteously pleaded with me to stop so he could recuperate, but well knowing the result should we linger, I shouted my warnings to him above the screaming of the storm, and when he reeled and even sank into the snow, I pulled him back upon his feet and forced him to move on.

Presently I felt myself overtaken by the same drowsiness that had enthralled Peoria Red, and a queer numbness which as it crept upwards from my feet seemed to kill my ambition to battle for life against the "Death of the Arctic."

Just as the last gleam of the blood-red sky which reflected the setting sun was swallowed up in the swirling masses of ice motes, Peoria Red sank beside the track, and although I tried everything to cause him to realize his danger if he failed to follow me, he keeled helplessly over into the snow, while a glassy stare in his half-shut eyes told me that he was doomed.

Then my own danger came home to me. Self-preservation is the first law of nature, and I promptly realized that to save my own life I must reach the section house, which I felt assured could not be many miles ahead of me, and where I would not only find shelter for myself, but perhaps obtain assistance to rescue my pal before it would be too late.

After taking one more farewell look at Peoria Red I made a step towards the track, but fell heavily to the ground. During the minutes I had lingered to save the life of my partner my feet seemed to have been turned into solid lead. I laughed aloud. As I was yet in full possession of my mental faculties this seemed to me a cruel joke, and I tried to arise so I could by stamping revive the circulation of the blood, but every time I arose half way I tumbled helplessly back into the snow. The desire to live increased, and when I felt the numbness creep from my limbs into my body, I crawled alongside Peoria Red and snuggled closely against him, hoping that our mutual body warmth would stave off the crisis to the last possible moment. He was groaning, and mustering the last vestige of control I yet had over my benumbed hands, I searched about in the darkness until I found his frozen fingers, and clasping them in my own I placed my mouth close to his ear and pleaded with him to bid me farewell. He was too far gone to speak, but twice a faint pressure against my frozen fingers told me that he had understood me, and I responded in the same manner. These were our farewells to each other in this world, a fitting finish to the tragedies of our toilful and thankless lives. I sank back into the snow and while I dreamily watched the snowflakes weave our spotless shroud, I dozed away and dreamed of those glorious, care-free days when I was yet with the "old folks" at home, chasing bright-hued butterflies in the warmth of the sunshine of youth and happiness.

The next thing I recall was a burning sensation in my throat, which involuntarily caused me to open my eyes. I felt as if I had slept for such a long time that all my faculties had become useless, for I could not, try as I might, utter a word or move a muscle, although to this day I vividly remember having heard a man, whom I could plainly see as he poured a steaming liquid into my open mouth, exclaim: "Thank God we are having better luck reviving this poor fellow than we had with the other one! Look, he has just opened his eyes, and listen, can you not hear him faintly groan?" Then I wandered back into dream-land—into a most dangerous delirium which lasted for several weeks and during which I hung as if by a mere thread, betwixt life and death.

When I recovered my reason, I found that I was domiciled in the bunk house, that together with the section house and tool house form the total of buildings upon every railroad "section" reservation. The foreman and his family resided in the section house, a two-story building; the tool house was used for storing the hand car and the track tools, while the bunk house, a small, one-story building, formed primarily the sleeping quarters, and secondly the social center of the section crew, whose five roughly dressed men were only permitted to enter the adjacent section house, where they boarded, at meal hours, as the foreman's home was at all other times considered by them a sort of hallowed spot. But the bunk house was their own, as within it they slept at night in the wooden "bunks", which were nailed one adjoining the other, all around the boarded walls, while in the center a small stove in which a roaring fire was kept up, made things comfortable for the inmates when they returned in the evenings after their day's work was done, and all day every Sunday--their day of rest.

While the men were absent and I was yet unable to attend to my needs, a sweet-faced lady looked after my wants and gave me my medicine. She was the foreman's wife, and her ever cheering words with never a sign of weariness that I, a sick and penniless harvester, should have so unexpectedly become a charge upon her hands, were most grateful to me.

I made inquiries among the laborers and ascertained from their answers that I was being cared for at the very section house that Peoria Red and I had striven to reach during the howling blizzard. I tried to find out what had become of my partner, but somehow they evaded my questions and it was many days before I managed by slow degrees to learn from them the facts concerning his absence.

During the height of the blizzard the foreman had ordered his crew out and upon their hand car driven at a lively rate by the power of the wind they had inspected every switch and car standing on sidings upon their section, to assure themselves that everything was properly safeguarded. While they were slowly "pumping" the hand car homeward, fighting against the force of the raging snow storm, they discovered us lying closely cuddled together, all but buried in the snow and beginning the eternal sleep of death. They stopped, and finding that we were yet faintly breathing, they loaded us upon the hand car and brought us to the section reservation.

When I Watched Baby Helen Repeat Her Evening Prayer, I Turned Away, for I Realized That I Missed That What is Most Sublime in All Creation: a Loving Wife and Devoted Mother; a Healthy Baby and one's Own 'Home, Sweet Home.'

Here by every means known to them they tried to revive the flickering sparks of life left in our frozen bodies. In my case they were successful, but Peoria Red, poor fellow, failed to respond to their heroic efforts. The following day they buried him on a slight elevation, diagonally across the track from the bunk house, where, whenever I looked in that direction, I could plainly discern the white board cross that the whole-souled laborers had erected to mark his grave.

The section foreman's name was Henry McDonald. He was a kind-hearted, yet stern man who demanded utmost obedience of those whom he commanded, while at the same time he was a loving father to his family. Foreman McDonald had none but the friendliest of greetings for me and he spent many moments at the bunk house trying to cheer me in my hard luck. Whenever I felt ill at ease for having added such a heavy burden to his small income, his quaint answer would always be: "Joe, what little we can do for you we would cheerfully do for any human being in distress. We do not ask for your excuses, as I feel that the Almighty above us will take care of me and my family, the pride of my humble life."

When I recovered some of my former strength I did the "chores" for the section foreman's wife, who not only boarded the five members of her husband's crew, but took proper care of her four healthy and ever hungry children.

The oldest one of them, a boy of sixteen, was named Donald. Then came a set of lively boy twins of fourteen, who had been baptized "Joseph" and "James", but who were for convenience called Joe and Jim. These twins resembled each other so closely that only their parents and intimate acquaintances could tell them apart. They were inseparable companions, and full of boyish mischief. The fourth child, the pet of everybody, was a beautiful, doll-like baby girl of three, whose name was Helen.

There was one singular imperfection about these children, that they had inherited from their father, which was a freak growth of an inch-wide streak of white hair which started from the center of their heads and continued downwards to the base of their skulls, and which as it showed plainly in their black hair made this strange birth-mark all the more conspicuous. Otherwise they were mentally, morally and physically perfect, and while I was convalescing I often stood by the window and watched them at play in the snow and it caused me to shudder every time I heard those youngsters shout with glee while they enjoyed the winter's sports, when I thought of poor Peoria Red whom this same merciless snow helped to murder.

In the evenings after supper had been served, I could see from the bunk house window how baby Helen in her sleeping room across the road in the section house knelt and humbly repeated her evening prayer, and then just before she was put to rest for the night, her father would kiss her "good-night", and as soon as he had left the room her sweet-faced mother would smother her with kisses before she tucked her darling between the spotless sheets of her cradle, and many were the times that I turned away from this picture of perfect domestic happiness as tears were welling into my eyes, for I realized that I had missed that which is most sublime in all creation:

A loving wife and devoted mother; a healthy baby and one's own "Home, sweet Home."

CHAPTER III.
"The Wreck."

Gradually I regained the use of my one-time totally frozen limbs, and when I felt myself able to do the severe labor required of men who toil upon a railroad section to earn their daily bread, I begged Foreman McDonald to allow me to work with his crew. I explained to him that this would be the greatest favor he could do for me, who found himself marooned many hundreds of miles from a city, without a job and penniless, in the midst of a bleak, snow-buried prairie. I also argued with him that to give me employment would be the easiest means for me to discharge my debt to him, which, although he absolutely refused to listen to any talk of indebtedness on my part, amounted to a tidy sum. He finally consented, and I commenced my task, fully equipped with warm clothes that were generously donated to me by my fellow laborers. The first time the pay-car stopped and the paymaster handed me my envelope I repaid Foreman McDonald every cent I owed him, and although this settled my financial indebtedness to him, the debt I owe him to this day for his timely help can never be repaid with mere coin.

One other time the pay-car stopped, and then the glad holidays of Christmas approached, and when the happy Yule-tide was just a week away, Foreman McDonald procured for each laborer a return pass to St. Paul. We went and made our Christmas purchases and returned after an absence of three days, each of us staggering under the weight of a heavily-laden sack which we carried slung over our backs, from the train into the bunk house.

Every spare minute until Christmas Eve there was a mysterious activity within the crowded space of the small bunk house. We were not only busy sorting over the purchases we had made in the big cities, which included a suitable present for each one of our foreman's family down to baby Helen, and one for each of the laborers, but we were kept busy keeping the youngsters from prying into the secrets which we did not wish to be revealed to them until Christmas Eve.

One of us had smuggled in a small Christmas tree, while another one had purchased the long whiskers that always go with a genuine "Santa Claus", so dear to the hearts of the children.

At last the natal feast of the Savior arrived, and to the complete surprise and delight of the McDonald family, we marched over to the foreman's home, led by old "Santa Claus", who in all his glory of a fur cap, long white hair and snowy whiskers, carried a wondrously decorated Christmas tree. We were royally welcomed, and after the Christmas tree's colored candles had been lighted and our presents had been distributed, we received those which had been purchased for us by the foreman and his thoughtful wife. Amidst the shouts of glee of the youngsters, and especially of Baby Helen, the hours flew past only too soon.

The time came for her to be put to bed, and the moment arrived for our depar-ture, but just before we went, the stern overseer of our work descended to the level of a satisfied father, and proudly permitted each one of us to kiss his baby's forehead, a most signal honor considering circumstances. As we were re-turning to our bunk house, he called from the porch of the section house, re-minding us to be sure to be in proper shape on the coming day to enjoy the best Christmas dinner that his wife, who was a very good cook, had ever placed be-fore guests.

No sooner had we entered our bunk house than we threw off all the restraint of etiquette which we had to observe at the "big" house, and quickly had a roaring fire in our stove, and while out of doors another blizzard was playing a tattoo upon the telegraph wires and was piling tons of snow upon the right of way, we had brewing in a pot upon the stove something that is not altogether in accor-dance with the tenets of temperance, but which meant additional cheer to us, whose thoughts were ever and anon slipping back to those days when we spent happy Christmas Eve's in very different surroundings. It was a curious fact, that although we celebrated till into the wee, small hours of the morning, when the first one of us crawled into his bunk it was only a few minutes until all of us had followed his example. We seemed to hate to be left alone.

About daybreak a loud pounding upon the door of our bunk house aroused us from our slumbers, and while we rubbed the drowsiness out of our eyes we heard Foreman McDonald calling to us to make haste, as a wrecking train was waiting to take us up the line to clear away a bad wreck.

It took little time for us to slip into our clothes, rush to the tool house and throw our track implements aboard the wrecker, and then climb into the coaches provided for our accommodation, in which were other section crews who had been picked up below us, and into which were loaded those for whom we stopped west of our reservation.

We had the right-of-track over every other train upon the line, and with six powerful engines pushing a snow-plow at full speed ahead of us, we reached our destination in almost record time, where we were put to work clearing away a serious wreck, which had been caused by a heavy passenger train running into a snow drift during a blinding blizzard, and having at the same time been de-railed from the tender back to the rear truck beneath the last sleeper. For three days and nights we worked like beavers, taking turns in eight hour shifts, sleep-ing and dining in the "bunk" cars attached to the wrecking train, shoveling away the solidly packed snow, "jacking" up the coaches, one at a time, and replacing the trucks upon the rails, and in the afternoon of the third day our combined ef-forts were rewarded, for amid the gladsome whistling of its engine the released train resumed its interrupted, eastbound journey.

We laborers were detained an additional day removing the wreckage, reloading the apparatus used and putting everything into a first-class condition for the resumption of the regular schedule. Then we boarded the wrecker to be distributed along the line.

The wrecking train's speed rapidly closed the gap of miles separating us from our reservation, and when at last—at about supper time—we entered upon our own section, we noted a satisfied sparkle in Foreman McDonald's eyes, when the cars, which had heretofore been lurching like ships at sea, spun with hardly a perceivable motion over the well attended road bed. Now the whistle blew for our section house; the brakes gripped the flanges of the wheels, and we gathered our belongings so as not to unnecessarily delay the others, and when the train stopped we soon had our track tools piled in front of our tool house. Then the wrecking train continued its journey, and while we stored our tools away we noted the disappointed look in our foreman's face when neither his wife nor any of his children came to greet him, or at least inquire as to the extent of the wreck, a most interesting item of gossip, considering the lonely location of our reservation.

When we had finished our task and the foreman had carefully locked the tool house, and while he walked towards the "big" house where not yet a single soul had opened the door to give him the usual glad greeting, although by the lamp that was illuminating the parlor we could see Mrs. McDonald and her children sitting about the heater, we hustled over to the bunk house, in which we quickly kindled a fire and then brought order out of the chaos we had left behind when we had been so unexpectedly called away to clear the track.

While we were thus busily engaged, our work was suddenly interrupted by several almost demoniacal shrieks that seemed to belong to Hades, and as if driven by some common impulse, we rushed pell mell out of doors and towards the "big" house. But before we could even reach it, we stopped short as if rooted into the ground, for there upon the front porch, with his face uplifted towards the starry firmament above him, stood Foreman McDonald, tearing like a raving maniac at the hairs of his head, while through the quietude of the night reverberated his heart-rending shrieks: "Oh God! Give me back my baby! Bring back my darling Helen! Merciful Father, do not punish me so cruelly as this!"

While we stood there wondering as to the causes of Foreman McDonald's strange pleading, his wife, pale as the snow, came from around the rear of the section house and begged us to take hold of Mr. McDonald to prevent him from harming himself, and when at this moment we saw the strong man sink into a corner of the porch and commence to pray aloud, we made a rush and after we took hold of him it required every bit of strength we six husky men could muster to restrain and drag him into the section house, where we stretched and tied him upon his bed and gave him narcotics that caused him to fall into a deep slumber.

Oh God! Give Me Back My Baby! Merciful Father, Do Not Punish Me So Cruelly As This!'

While we sat about his bed watching his every move, poor Mrs. McDonald repeated to us, amid heart-racking sobs, the dire calamity that had overtaken her happy family since our departure. That Helen, the pet of the family and of the rough section men, had disappeared from her home, leaving not a trace. Further questioning elicited from the distracted mother this information:

The blizzard had given way to a perfectly calm afternoon, and after they had enjoyed their Christmas dinners, Mrs. McDonald had watched Helen toddle behind her brothers to where the passing siding turned away from the main line, permitting a small pond to form, which, being smooth as glass and swept clear of snow by the storm, offered a splendid opportunity to try out their new skates, which they had received amongst their presents.

The youngsters were altogether too busy enjoying their rare sport to pay heed to their baby sister, and when darkness approached they scampered back to the house where they told their mother of the good time they had had. Her first question, however, was concerning the whereabouts of little Helen, as she quickly noted her absence from the returning children. "Boys, where have you left your little sister?" "Why, mother," readily replied Donald, her eldest son, "Helen must have been back to the house long ago, as we have not seen her since she watched us put on our new skates."

Tormented by a mother's instinct which told her that all was not well with her child, Mrs. McDonald, assisted by her sons, made a thorough search of the house, thinking that perhaps the baby might have toddled back to its home, tired of watching her brothers skate upon the pond, and had, unobserved by her mother, entered one of the bed rooms and gone to sleep. Carefully she looked through every room and then she searched the whole building from cellar to garret, all the while loudly calling for her missing darling, but the search proved futile.

Then she lit lanterns, one for herself and one for each of her boys, and together they searched through the bunk house, the tool house and every other out-building on the reservation, but all their hunting was of no avail, as they found no trace of the child.

Up and down the right-of-way they searched, hoping to find the tracks in the soft snow showing the direction the tot might have taken, but every effort was in vain, and they had almost reached the garden gate of the house, all of them broken-heartedly weeping, having given up all hope of ever hearing again of their Helen, when "Spot", the shepherd dog, the playmate of the children, came racing towards them, swinging a rag, that he held between his sharp teeth, playfully about his head. He had been awakened by his mistress's calls for her child, and the lighted lanterns they carried had fooled the intelligent canine into reasoning that this was to be a prolongation of the Christmas festivities of the preceding night, and he had promptly entered into the spirit of the game.

Mrs. McDonald called the dog to her side, and examined the supposed rag the beast had played with, and found it to be the first clue that she had thus far discovered, as it was little Helen's red flannel undergarment. Reeling but upheld by the thought that she might not yet be too late, poor Mrs, McDonald ordered her boys to take securely hold of Spot, and then she ran as fast as her fright and weakened feet would carry her, to the dog's house, but its interior and the usual slim appearance of the watch dog, disproved the terrible notion which had caused her to make the hasty trip, that Spot had made a meal of her baby. Grateful from the bottom of her heart for even this small relief in her terrible perdicament, she rejoined her boys, and as sort of forlorn hope, she rubbed Helen's tiny garment against the dog's nose, and ordered the collie to go and find the missing child.

The intelligent animal seemed to understand what was demanded of him, for presently, whining as if to appeal to them to go with him, he rushed forward, and as they followed he led them to the pond, then across the tracks where he stopped by a small pile of clothes, which proved to be every stitch of little Helen's garments—shoes, stockings and all, with the sole exception of a tiny gold locket containing her parents' pictures, which Mrs. McDonald had hung by its gold chain around the baby's neck, and the red flannel garment that the dog had brought to their attention, no doubt considering it a most welcome plaything.

Back to the section house she dragged herself carrying the tiny garments. Arriving there, she carefully questioned the boys and brought out only one more useless item, that a westbound immigrant train had pulled into the siding to permit an eastbound passenger train to pass them.

For four seemingly endless days the poor mother with her three small boys helplessly waited for someone to assist her, her husband and all the other men having gone to the wreck. Telephones were unknown in those days, and with no strong hands to pump the heavy hand car through the foot-high snow that now covered the track, there was nothing else to do but to hope, as she did not dare send one of her sons to the nearest village, not knowing at what moment a blizzard might add another calamity to her burden of woe. In all those long days, until the released passenger train flew past, not a single train passed up or down the line, so all she and her children could do was to weep and wait for her husband's return, to whom she then told all the circumstances of the child's disappearance, which affected him far more than she thought it would be possible.

After she had finished her sad story she asked us to give her our opinion as to the cause of the baby's disappearance. One of our men had the most likely solution of the riddle as he thought that the baby had watched her brothers discard their overcoats, and later their coats, as the exercise while skating warmed them, and Helen, childlike, thinking this the proper thing, had in a playful mood discarded her clothes, intending to skate barefooted upon the glistening ice, and finding that the cold snow hurt her feet, and being unable to don her garments, had wandered out upon the bleak prairie and had been frozen to death, the fate that had overtaken Peoria Red and so many strong men.

Leaving one man to act as nurse to the foreman, we others returned to the bunk house, as Mr. McDonald's heavy and regular breathing assured us that he would at least rest peacefully until the following morning.

He Would Dig With His Bare Hands Deep into the Cruel
Snow, Searching for His Lost Baby—His Own Little Helen.

For several days, undaunted by constant failures to accomplish anything, we carefully searched the right of way and the prairie for our pet, and had Spot, the collie, assist us, but finally were forced to believe that little Helen had departed for the land of the Angels.

In the evenings, to while away the hours and to be in readiness when in the Spring the warm rays of the sun would remove the snowy shroud and reveal to us her mortal remains, we constructed a small coffin, that we carefully painted a somber black, and we also whittled another white cross, which should in due time mark her eternal resting place.

For weeks Foreman McDonald raved in a high fevered delirium, but gradually, assisted by the railroad company's physician, who made frequent calls at the section house, and the loving aid and attention of his ever faithful wife, he rallied so far that he again became able to take us out on the track and personally direct our work.

Night after night, for months after her disappearance, when our supper had been served at the big house, and we had returned to the bunk house and had blown out the lamp before retiring, the stern foreman, now only a broken hearted father, yearning for his own sweet baby girl, would slip noiselessly, and he thought unobserved, out of the front door of the section house, and slink stealthily to the very spot where his darling's tiny garments had been found, and there amid heart-rending shrieks, which we in our bunk house could plainly hear above the weird moanings of the winter storms, he would dig with his bare hands deep into the cruel snow, searching for his lost baby—his own little Helen.

As Spring approached the warming rays of the sun finally conquered the thick snow blanket that covered the landscape, and led by our foreman we carefully searched the prairie, praying to be permitted to give at least a human burial to his daughter's earthly remains, but it nearly wrecked his mind when even this privilege was denied him, as we found not a trace of the child.

Then, hoping to lighten somewhat the fearful burden of woe borne by her parents, we placed those last mementos of her brief visit upon earth into the little black coffin that we had constructed, and gave the baby's garments a solemn burial alongside the mound of my partner, Peoria Red, and above the new mound we erected the other white cross to keep company with the first one, and tell its silent story to the passengers who flew past aboard swift trains, that two pitiful tragedies had been enacted at this lone section reservation within the short span of a few months.

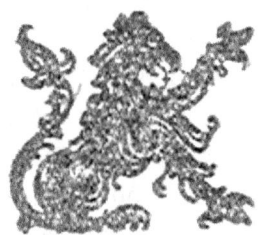

CHAPTER IV.
"The Drifter".

And Spring came back to the Northland. The trees and bushes commenced to bud. As if by magic the brown winter tints of the water and frost bogged prairie were transformed into a daintily colored green carpet by the sprouts that the slumbering grasses sent forth into the balmy air, while here and there a venturesome flower spread its multi-colored petals towards the warming rays of the sun, and lastly the song birds, the infallible sign of nature's complete resurrection, came home from the Southland and rebuilt their storm-torn nests amid the warbling of gladsome notes, their jubilee song of happiness and satisfaction.

With these signs of the re-awakening of Nature there came to me the strange "Call of the Road". Heretofore it had never come as strongly as it came at this time, when after a long and monotonous winter's toil the rattling trains as they shot over our section, the darting birds as they foraged their subsistence, and even the thumping of the wheels under our hand car seamed to beckon me to follow their example and move away. Although I tried with might and main to resist its call, gradually the bunk house became a dungeon, the endless prairie a prison, and the Dakotas themselves became entirely too small to hold me, and when the pay car stopped to hand me my month's wages, I could no longer withstand the temptation to follow the "Call of the Road" and be up and gone. It was a hard matter for me to bid Foreman McDonald and his family farewell, and the last promise I made before I left was, that should circumstances permit I would find my way back in the fall to again take my place with the section crew, that until then would be held open for my return.

I drifted to Saint Paul and then down to hustling St. Louis, and from there to beautiful San Antonio, and when the binders cut wide swaths into the ripening, top-heavy, golden grain on the banks of the Rio Grande, I found myself back in my chosen element, toiling long hours during the day in the harvest field, and then until way into the night dancing the fantastic fandango with dark eyed Mexican Senoritas, to the accompaniment of twanging guitars and squeaking mouth organs, and staking my come-easy, go-easy earnings against the "Monte" layouts dealt by swift-handed Mexican Senores, who had crossed the river from the Mexican side for the double purpose of helping to harvest the wheat and trimming, by means of "sure thing" games, the American harvesters.

Then came the harvest dance, the festival which indicated that upon the ranch the harvest had been finished, and that I was no longer wanted. So I drifted northward, following the ripening wheat, ever toiling, ever squandering, and always attending the harvest dance which celebrated my exit.

When the inclement weather set in, for want of something better to do, I drifted back towards the lone prairie section reservation to take my place in the ranks of those who tamp the ties and tighten the "fish-plates," which hold the rails together.

I had hoboed a freight train as far as the water tank, that stood a scant six miles east of the section reservation, and now I walked leisurely through familiar scenery towards my former winter home, hoping every minute to surprise Foreman McDonald and his crew at work on the track. That day, however, they happened to be repairing on the other end of the section, so I managed to slip unobserved up to the front door of the "big" house, where intending to surprise Mrs. McDonald by my unexpected return, I knocked on the front door. To our mutual delight Mrs. McDonald opened the door, and after giving me a glad welcome, asked me into the house. She soon had one of her best meals steaming in front of me, having correctly surmised that a man riding freight trains and walking six miles, needed a hearty repast. Although I was more than anxious to inquire about many items of interest, especially if my long journey had not been made in vain, as my place might have been filled by some other fellow in search of employment, she seemed to completely ignore my presence, for she was only in the dining room during the brief moments when she placed the filled plates upon the table.

I finished my dinner, and then, uninvited by Mrs. McDonald, but just as she had taught me a year ago, when I helped her to do the chores about the house while convalescing from my freezing experience, I carried the soiled dishes into the kitchen. Noticing that she was still in full mourning, I made careful inquiries as to whether any trace had been found of the missing child during my absence, to which she sadly replied that nothing had ever become of the land-wide search that had been made. Her apparent reticence caused my curiosity to mount high, and I followed up my question by pleasantly inquiring as to Foreman McDonald's present state of health. She looked at me with an expression of terror in her eyes, as if my words had stabbed her to her heart, but did not answer, and a moment later she could not answer had she wanted to, for heart-broken sobs choked her voice, but she beckoned to me to follow her to the front porch and there she pointed her trembling finger in the direction where they had buried my pal, Peoria Red, and there I could plainly see three small, white crosses. Steeled by the many other woes that she had during a long and dreary year borne with fortitude, she temporarily overcame her weakness, and with a clear voice she counted: "One, two, three," and then the poor woman paused, it seemed the strain had almost been too much for her, and then in a faltering, almost inaudible voice she continued: "Peoria Red, Helen McDonald, Henry McDonald," and then collapsed.

I carried her limp, unconscious form into the parlor, and after some efforts managed to bring her out of the faint, and when she had fully recovered so as to withstand the ordeal, she slowly repeated to me the story of her summer's experience, how Foreman McDonald, unable to be without his Helen, had wasted to a shadow of his former self; and in August had died of a broken heart, and how only the thoughts that upon her own frail self had now devolved the duty to provide for their three small sons had given her the strength to resolve not to succumb to a like fate. Her voice brightened when she told me that in all her misery there had come one tiny streak of good fortune to her, a poor, helpless widow cast upon the mercy of the world with three children. The new section foreman, whom the company had sent to fill the vacancy caused by Mr. McDonald's death, proved to be a crusty, old bachelor of perhaps sixty-five who no doubt appreciating a few extra comforts at his age, gladly consented to have Mrs. McDonald remain and continue taking charge of the section house, and the boarding crew, in return for a small stipend and a shelter for herself and her fatherless children.

When in the evening the new foreman and the crew came home from their work, Mrs. McDonald spoke a word in my favor, and although there was no need of an additional laborer, the new foreman, after he had heard my story, engaged my services.

Until the thawing of the snow I faithfully worked upon the section, but when Spring again set in with full force, there came another attack of the strange fever that drove me onward every year, and, following the "Call of the Wanderlust", I left for the South, having again promised that with the approach of winter I would be on hand to fill my place with the section crew.

I drifted along with the harvest, but after the wintry storms that swept over the endless expanse of the plains had twisted off the last leaves which the autumn had burnished to a fiery red, and the nights became too chilly to make out-of-door camping a pleasure, I found my way back to my North Dakota section reservation, which I now considered my regular winter quarters.

I arrived at the section house almost at the time when the hand car was due to return for supper, and intending to surprise Mrs. McDonald, knowing that in all the world it would be the poor widow who would give me, a homeless harvester, a glad welcome, I slipped almost noiselessly up to the porch and knocked on the door, but no answer came to my repeated knocks. Then I tried to open the door, which during Foreman McDonald's time had never been known to be locked, and to my surprise I found it bolted. Thinking that perhaps the widow had gone to purchase provisions, I walked around to the rear of the building and tried every door, but found that all of them were locked. A miserably starved black cat, that made a ten foot leap when she first espied me, was the only sign of life on the place, while the many rag-stuffed broken window panes plainly indicated that great changes had been made at the "big" house since my last departure. There was something uncanny in the silence about the place, and a strange gloom seemed to have settled over everything that foreboded to me only evil happenings.

For want of something better I resolved to await the return of the section crew from their day's work, and walked back to the front of the house and took a seat upon the steps. I casually glanced across the tracks to where my pal, Peoria Red, was sleeping his eternal sleep, and I was almost stunned by surprise when instead of the three crosses which I had left behind when in the Spring I drifted to the Southland, I counted five of those ill-omened messengers of death. In vain I tried to solve the riddle of these added graves, and was about to cross over to the grave plot beyond the tracks, hoping to find some inscriptions upon the new crosses that would give me a key to the new tragedies that I knew must have caused their presence, when the hand car with the returning crew came into view, and forgetting all other matters, I walked down to the tool house to meet it and was soon cordially welcomed by my old comrades who had "held down" their jobs through the hot summer months.

I Walked Around to the Rear of the Building Where a Miserably Starved Cat, That Made a Ten Foot Leap when She First Espied Me, Was the only Sign of Life on the Place.

The same foreman, who had taken Foreman McDonald's place was still in charge of the section reservation, and he good naturedly ordered the crew to take proper care of me at the bunk house, where quickly a hot supper, which the laborers cooked and served themselves, was made ready, a welcome meal for a man who had not tasted a mouthful since the early morning.

After supper had been cleared away and everything had been made snug about the house, my chance came to inquire why I had found everything about the reservation topsy-turvy, as compared with former days, and I especially inquired as to the well-being and whereabouts of Mrs. McDonald and her three youngsters, and the following is the information one of the laborers gave me:

Mrs. McDonald, with the assistance of her three sons, who had grown into strong lads, had given to the crew of the section house the same motherly care that characterized those days when yet her husband's presence and praises spurred her on to make her best efforts. Every school day she saw her boys ride off to the school house in the early morning upon ponies she had purchased for them, as the school was five miles south from the railroad.

Amid the work of the household and the enjoyment that her three sturdy sons gave her, as they fairly adored their mother and did everything to cause her to forget the sorrowful past, gradually the deathly pallor of Mrs. McDonald's face and the lusterless eyes with their heavy black rings beneath them, gave way to red cheeks and the same brilliancy that were hers when she was yet the proud mother of baby Helen. Some days, especially when the darkness had hidden those ominous crosses from her vision, she would sing the songs she used to sing in the days of her happiness, which showed to us rough laborers the fight this weak woman was waging with herself trying to forget, for the sake of her sons, those many sad days which had been hers, so that her mourning for things that had been, would not embitter their future.

Almost unawares the Summer followed the Spring, and soon came the glad days for the school children—the annual vacation of the schools—and the three sons of Mrs. McDonald came home to rest from their studies. Gradually unrest, especially in Joe and Jim, the twins, could be noted, as they found time hanging heavily upon their hands. They begged the foreman to permit them to work with the section crew during the months of their vacation, but as they had not sufficient strength to do the strenuous work required of a section laborer, the foreman had to refuse their request. Then they tried to find employment amongst the scattered ranches which here and there commenced to break the monotony of the prairie, but as the planting had been finished long ago, and the harvest would not commence until after school had re-opened, their appeals were in vain. Then they discovered that we had stacked a lot of useless, decayed railroad ties in the backyard of the section house, and they reduced these into stove lengths. After this task had been finished, despair seemed to have taken hold of the boys as there was nothing for them to do to occupy their time.

Idleness breeds mischief. One morning when their good mother wondered why Joe and Jim did not show up at the breakfast table, she sent Donald, her eldest boy, upstairs to arouse them. He returned and reported that they were not in their room. Her hasty investigation proved that they had not only not occupied their beds, and their savings bank had been emptied of its contents, but the broken-hearted mother was nearly frantic when she found that her thoughtless sons had disappeared without leaving even a short note apprising her of their intentions, or at least bidding her a brief farewell.

This was the last and most cruel blow an unkind fate had inflicted upon poor, suffering Mrs. McDonald, and it was days before they were sure that she would not succumb. In the meantime the foreman and every other friend of the sorrow-stricken widow put every bit of legal and police nachinery they could command into motion, trying to find at least a trace of the twins, and although for weeks they searched far and wide, not a single clue as to their whereabouts was found, nor was a single line or letter received from them by their mother, who prayed for weeks for this favor of Heaven, while at the same time her very appearance, her returned pallor and her lusterless eyes told far better than any words how this last calamity was slowly but none the less certainly eating out her heart.

It was almost a month after their disappearance that the bereaved, helpless and hopeless mother received her first clue as to her sons whereabouts. A freight train had been held up on the siding on account of a bad washout, and the crew, finding itself short of provisions had come up to the section house and had requested Mrs. McDonald to prepare for them a meal. While they were dining, one of the brakemen caused Mrs. McDonald to fall into a dead faint when he in a rough but jocular way remarked to her: "I bet you, Mrs. McDonald, that your Joe and Jim are having the time of their lives down in Minneapolis, as I haven't seen them around the reservation since the night I found them hoboing my train into Grand Forks, although our train has passed through here many times since that day. They told me then that they were bound for the "Twin Cities" to pick up a fortune. Have you heard from them lately, Mrs. McDonald? Are they prospering?"

The police authorities of Saint Paul and Minneapolis were notified, and although correspondence was exchanged, nothing was accomplished. For two more months Mrs. McDonald waited in vain, hoping against hope that at least they would send a letter to appease her piteous fears as to their fates, while in the meantime she faded away to a mere shadow of her former self, and then suddenly decided to quit the reservation forever. It seemed as if she wished to tear herself away from the place which had brought to her such merciless misfortune. She decided to move into Canada, in those days a newly discovered Eldorado, to which all those turned who were willing to work and to hustle while tempting fickle fortune.

On the evening preceding the day Mrs. McDonald and Donald were to depart, after we had finished our suppers, we presented her with a purse of fifty dollars, that we had made up among ourselves, as a token of the high esteem in which we held the unfortunate woman, and too, to assist and cheer her on the journey into an unknown land. Then we filed back to our bunk house, and while we sat about its single room, the gloom that seemed to hold us, spoiled all desire to open a conversation, as the widow's departure meant the loss of one who had been almost a mother to us rough and homeless laborers. Just as we made ready to retire someone knocked on the bunk house door, and thinking that perhaps some wandering tramp had the nerve to bother us at this late hour in the night, we roughly ordered the intruder to be gone. Instead of going, the knocks continued, and angry at the persistence of the person, we pulled the door open, and to our complete surprise found that it was Mrs. McDonald who had knocked for admission. Realizing the great honor she was conferring upon us, we politely bade her to enter and asked her to be seated. She was attired in the dress in which she intended to make the journey on the following day, and its sombre black of deepest mourning, aided by the yellow light of our lamp, transformed the pallor of her haggard face into an almost ghastly white. We patiently waited for her to open the conversation, of course expecting that she had come to thank us once more for having presented her with the purse. It was some time before she could find her voice and then in the saddest tone that weaver heard, she begged of us strong men, as the last favor she would ever ask of us, to make for her two more white crosses, the same as stood above the other graves, and to deliver them to her in the early morning, and then, as if this last humble request had completely shattered her nerves, she tottered, an almost lifeless wreck, out into the moonlit night.

None of us uttered a single word, it seemed we had been stunned by the solemnity of the poor widow's request, but we opened the bunk house door to see that no harm befell her upon her trip back to the "big" house. To our surprise, instead of going to the section house she tottered over to where Foreman McDonald lay buried, and we saw her pray long and earnestly by the little mound that held his remains; then she arose and wearily dragged herself to the place by the railroad track where little Helen's garments had been found, and here once more she sank upon her knees in prayer, and then staggered back towards the "big" house, where, just before she entered the gate of the fence surrounding the yard, she knelt a third time to utter a prayer. While we silently stood and watched and pitied the poor broken-hearted woman, she heavily keeled over. We rushed to her side to give her assistance, and found she had fainted away, but in her unconsciousness she muttered the words "Joe" and "Jim", and we readily understood for whom her last farewell prayer had been offered.

We carried her into the section house where we revived her, and then we returned to the bunk house and until late into the night sawed, hammered and whittled those two crude crosses into shape, supposing Mrs. McDonald intended to take them with her into Canada, to keep as a memento of her sad experiences.

In the morning after we had been served with breakfast, we handed her the crosses which we had carefully wrapped in paper so that upon her journey their ominous outlines would not recall unpleasant memories and cause her needless anguish. Then we went back to the bunk house to await the arrival of the train and assist in loading aboard the bagggage that Mrs. McDonald was to take with her into Canada. Only a few minutes had elapsed, when to our surprise, the foreman called us to the door and commanded us to follow him, Mrs. McDonald and Donald, who carried the two crosses we had made for his mother.

We followed them to the little graveyard upon the right-of-way, and while we stood by bareheaded, frail Mrs. McDonald planted the two new crosses at equal distances from the other three, and we saw that upon one of them was written "James" and upon the other "Joseph." After she had scattered prairie flowers over all the graves, we offered up silent prayers, and then with not a single dry eye in our sad procession, we returned to the reservation.

In the afternoon we flagged the westbound passenger train, and after wishing her God speed, we tenderly placed the sobbing widow and Donald aboard, bound for the then little known and undeveloped western section of Canada, and when the tail end of the train passed us, a sportily dressed fellow, who, with other passengers, was sitting upon the observation platform of the last Pullman, upon perceiving those plain, white crosses, which glared so conspicuously above the green sward of the prairie to the right of the train, while he pointed his finger derisively in their direction, made some remarks to the other passengers, and laughed. He did not know the story of the tragic events which caused their presence nor that under four of the little crosses the hopes and happiness of poor Mrs. McDonald lay buried.

CHAPTER V.
"The Call of the City."

It was the "Call of the City", the true brother of that other curse of humanity, the "Call of the Road", that had been heard by Joe and Jim. For years previous to their unannounced departure they had felt its subtle influence when they read about the grand city in the newspapers which were occasionally found upon the right-of-way, having been thrown there from the passing trains by passengers who had read them. The "call" had also come to them while listening to the stories of adventure among the wonderful palaces and the sodden slums which comprise every city, which were told them by passing tramps as they stopped to rest, to ask for employment, or more often to beg food at the section house. But the strongest incentive of all was the hoboes, who as they passed by aboard of freight trains, with their feet dangling out of open box car doors or hanging to the mail and express cars of passenger trains, waved friendly greetings to the lads, which they interpreted as a beckoning to the city.

Except for the rare instances, when the railroad company transferred their father to take charge of some other section, or the few times when they had made trips to the nearest villages, which were small and had but few inhabitants, the McDonald boys had never seen another world except the one whose boundaries melted into the endless, undulating prairie around their home.

Their parents, who were ever worrying about how to properly provide for their family, had—as nowadays so many other parents do—entirely overlooked the fact that growing boys should be permitted to travel, even if only upon an excursion, to curb within them the inborn and almost irresistible desire to roam, which all have inherited from ancestors, who attired in wooden shoes and coarse apparel, and carrying gunny sacks, had landed not so many years ago at Castle Garden, after having crossed the stormy Atlantic in the steerage of a sailing vessel, and who instead of bringing along a fancy "family tree", had brought with them a pair of calloused, but willing hands, intending to win with them a way to wealth and fame, in the New World, for their own humble selves and their "proud" descendants.

The "Call of the City" found in the twins willing listeners as the cessation of their school duties, the enforced idleness at the reservation, and the monotony of their existence became a bane to them. They hearkened to the call that had already conquered a vast army of other boys, sons of those who till the soil and labor out-of-doors earning a fair competence, which although it demands hard toil, gives in exchange pure air, healthy food and every comfort and luxury that willing hands backed by intelligence can produce.

For months prior to their departure on their trip, whenever they could gallop beyond ear shot of their elder brother, while riding to and from school, and at night when alone in their bedroom, Joe and Jim pictured to each other the grand future which they thought every city offered to them, comparing it favorably with the drudge of the life of monotonous toil that would be theirs at the section reservation. They repeated the stories of success they had read in the newspapers, the magazines and even in their school books, which told in glowing words of poor lads who had forsaken the country to become rich and famous in the cities, but they never repeated, for they had never read the stories of those unaccountable numbers who had "moved to town" and who had been swallowed up by the city's whirlpool, to become slaves of the mills and the factories, serfs of the bars and the counters, and who had been forced to toil from dawn to dusk to barely eke out an existence that meant residing high up in the simmering, sweltering tenements, or in damp, pest-ridden basements, deep down in the bowels of the earth, which coupled with improper food, quickly reduced their vitality, so that although they were young in years, the merciless lash of the city's fight for a living had bent their backs and prematurely aged them.

Joe and Jim realized that it would have been an impossibility for them to wring from their mother her consent to let them try their luck in the city, for since their father's death, they had become her moral support. They felt ashamed to be loafing idly about the reservation until school opened again and have their widowed mother support them, as they were now sixteen years of age, and more than able to support not only themselves, but could and would gladly have supported her had an opportunity been offered them. The more they argued the matter between themselves, the more they became resolved to journey to some city, and at least until the time came for them to be on hand at school opening, make their own way and perhaps their fortune, which seemed to them within easy reach. They had saved almost fifty dollars, which had been earned running errands and working as water-boys whenever an "extra" gang had been sent from the division point to assist their father's crew in putting in a new culvert, building a new switch or doing other heavy work requiring more man-power then the reservation crew could supply. This money was kept in a small savings bank, to which they had easy access.

Their scheming and plotting had finally reached the point where it needed only the least provocation to cause them to skip, and this chance came to them one evening while the section crew was in their bunk house, and their mother and Donald, whom they had not taken into their confidence, were busy in the kitchen, when a long, eastbound freight train pulled in upon the siding to let the westbound passenger train pass it. The boys were lounging in the front yard and as the freight train slowly drew past them they espied some open, empty box cars, and as if driven by some strange impulse, they pressed each other's hands and whispered that now "the time had come," and then dashed up to their room, emptied the savings bank, packed their few necessities into small bundles and, carefully avoiding the rear of the section house where the kitchen was located, and keeping on the alert to prevent meeting or being seen by any of the section men or train crew, they ran down the side of the train, which was just pulling out of the siding, climbed—as they had so often seen hoboes do—into an empty box car, and slinking back into the darkness of its farthest corner, they were soon traveling beyond familiar landscape. Gradually they became accustomed to the jolting and rattling of their side-door Pullman and stretched themselves upon its hard floor and fell asleep.

They Were Aroused from their Slumbers by the Bright Rays Shed by a Lantern Held by a Brakeman Who Discovered them in the Box Car.

It must have been almost morning when, as they stopped at the last water tank west of Grand Forks, they were aroused from their slumbers by the bright rays shed by a lighted lantern held in the hands of a brakeman who roughly shouted: "Which way, kids?" "To Saint Paul," answered Joe. "Got some money, lads, with which you can square your ride?" inquired the railroad man, as he raised his lantern higher so he could the better estimate the fare he could charge his hobo-passengers, who had now risen and were rubbing their sleep-laden eyes, and then he recognized the twins, whom he had so often greeted from his passing train, and added: "Well, I will be danged if you hoboes aren't Widow McDonald's twins," and then, after he had questioned them as to their destination, and while he withdrew his lantern from the door, he finished the conversation by excusing himself: "It's all right, my lads," he cheerfully said, "all charges have been settled as we brakemen do not collect toll from friends. It's the hoboes we are after to make them 'hit the grit'." and with that he was gone.

A few hours later they landed at Grand Forks, N.D., and by keeping close to their side-door Pullman they had the luck to reach, unmolested, the outskirts of Minneapolis on the evening of the third day after leaving their home.

When the freight train slowed up to pull into the railroad yards, imitating the other hoboes whom they saw diving out of all sorts of hiding places, they jumped to the ground, scaled the right-of-way fence and made a bee line for the wonder of all wonders, that they had read, heard and dreamed so much about —"The City."

CHAPTER VI.
"The Golden Rule Hotel."

It required some moments before the boys became accustomed to the strange sights which spread themselves out before their wondering eyes. The speed and the clanging of the horse-drawn street cars, the shouts of the teamsters, the gas lamps, which now as darkness was approaching were lit, while the brilliantly illuminated saloons, the gayly decorated windows of the stores and shops, in fact everything seemed to them a far different world from the one they had just left behind them upon the bleak prairie.

They walked about the streets until they felt that they must find a shelter for the night, but being afraid to accost one of the many strangers who rushed past them and who not even deigned to cast a glance at the open-mouthed lads who marvelled at the people's haste to be gone, they tackled a gaudily uniformed policeman. "Yes, my lads," the good-natured guardian of the peace explained to them, after he had noted their red-bandana wrapped bundles and that their suits were somewhat the worse for their three days riding in the box car, "you of course do not wish to stop at the Windsor, the highest classed hotel in Minneapolis, but I think that I know the proper place for you, it's the 'Golden Rule Hotel', the best place in our city for lads like you." And then he directed them so they could easily find the hotel, and as a parting word, told them that it was a most reasonably priced place, as they charged only fifteen cents for a night's lodging, and then finished his fatherly advice by adding, that every cent saved meant a cent gained.

They followed the officer's instructions, and within a short time found the "Golden Rule Hotel". They entered its office, a spacious well-kept room, but the next moment they were almost frightened out of their shoes by the loathsome sight which met their eyes, as they found themselves in the midst of a lot of cursing, semi-sober harvesters; crippled, alcohol-marked vagrants; blind mendicants; drunkards and blackguards, in fact a choice collection of the most degraded specimens of humanity.

James nudged Joe and whispered: "Brother Joe, this is no place for fellows like we are. No place for lads who have come to seek employment. Let's get out of here as quickly as we can and hunt a different lodging house." Joe, who acted as the treasurer, having in mind the sum that they could save by stopping at a reasonably-priced lodging place, calmed his brother's fears by replying: "Wait and see what sort of a place this is. The company may not exactly suit us, but has not the policeman told us that this is the best hotel in Minneapolis for us, and look, Jim, doesn't this office look rather inviting?" While they yet argued the point, the manager of the hotel, an oily-faced fellow, accosted them: "Strangers in Minneapolis, eh?" he queried, with utmost kindness, while at the same time his shifty eyes scanned the country-style suits they wore. "I welcome you to our hustling city, and invite you to make your headquarters at the "Golden Rule Hotel" during your stay." Noting that the lads were yet undecided what to do and correctly surmising that they had received an old-fashioned, Christian home training, he suavely added: "Our charges are most reasonable, only fifteen cents per night, and every Sunday morning we hold here in the office a most beautiful song and prayer service, and I am sure you lads will be glad to join us in singing grand hymns."

This last statement settled the whole matter, for the twins felt that a place in which prayer meetings were held and holy hymns chanted could never be an unfit place for the likes of them, and instead of landing in a "hobo-joint" as they had first feared, they concluded that they had actually struck a home. Perceiving the splendid impression his appeal had made upon the newcomers, the manager almost pushed the lads before the counter and made them write their names upon the soiled and tattered register. Then he explained to them that the charge was fifteen cents for one night's lodging, but if they wished to settle in advance by the week only seventy-five cents would be the rate. Seeing that he could save sixty cents, Joe paid for each a week's lodging. They left their bundles in the manager's care, and then inquired for a reasonable priced restaurant, to which they went and satisfied their appetites.

It was nearly midnight when they found their way back to the "Golden Rule Hotel", whose manager was waiting their return, and who explained to them that as every "room" was taken he was anxious to show them to their "beds", so he could lock the hotel and retire for the night. He lighted the stub of a candle, and telling the boys to follow him, he led them up a creaky stairway. Higher and higher he mounted, and when the twins thought he must have almost reached the roof, he opened a small door, and picking his way by the flickering light of the candle between wooden partitions, he at last stopped in front of two unoccupied bunks, one above the other, and after telling his surprised guests that these were the "beds" for which they had paid, and after cautioning them to blow out the candle as soon as possible, he bade them good-night and vanished into the darkness, and a moment later the slamming of a door below them told the lads that they were virtually prisoners, as the hotel had been locked for the night.

"Joe," whispered Jim to his brother, after both had inhaled several whiffs of the foul atmosphere into their lungs, which had heretofore only been accustomed to breathing the pure air of the prairie, "in what sort of an inferno have we landed?" And then he held the candle high, and by its unsteady, sickly-yellow light he counted five bunks, one above the other, in the tier they were to sleep, built from the floor right up to the ceiling, with only sufficient space intervening for a human being to crawl into. These vertical tiers of bunks looked for all the world like boarded up book shelves in a library, one adjoining the other as far as their eyes could penetrate the darkness of the hall, and in each and every bunk was a snoring human wretch, while the suffocating atmosphere caused by the overcrowding and the insufficient ventilation, which was greatly enhanced by the heat of the summer, made the "Golden Rule Hotel" an absolutely unfit place for human habitation.

"Let's get out of this horrid place, even if we have to sleep upon the chairs down below in the office," whispered Jim; but before he could add another word or make a move to leave the hall, a threatening voice, emanating from the tier of bunks in the darkness behind them, whose owner had evidently been disturbed by their conversation, roughly commanded them to "hush up and blow out the candle."

Unused to the ways of the city, the frightened boys obeyed the command, and after they had undressed in the darkness, they climbed into the bunks and being tired out by their sight-seeing, they were soon asleep.

In the early morning, after they had made their toilets by an open faucet to which a cake of perforated laundry soap had been chained, they descended to the office and there demanded of the manager the return of the money they had paid for their week's lodging, less the cost of the lodging of the preceding night, but this worthy not only absolutely refused to refund a single cent, but derided them so for being "Reubens" that they decided to stop, just for spite, at the "Golden Rule Hotel" until they received their money's worth.

After a hasty breakfast, they copied from the want columns of the Minneapolis Tribune, the best paper in the city, the addresses of those who had inserted advertisements which the twins thought would suit them, and set out to search for a job, that they had long ago planned should form the first stepping stone towards the fortune and the fame they had resolved to gather in the city.

It is an easy job for someone who has had experience in this line to find employment in a city. Many a bright city chap quits his job in the evening to be almost certain to pick up a new one the following morning. But for Joe and Jim, filled as they were with childish dreams of easy fortune, it was a far different matter, especially while they had dollars clinking in their jeans, as a boy possessing plenty of loose change is mighty particular about the employment he accepts, so, although the lads hunted high and low, from early till late, they could not find suitable places, and after supper they returned to the "Golden Rule Hotel" to "roost" again in their bunks, surrounded by those occupied by the riff-raff of the slums.

Joe and Jim were awakened the following morning by the racket the rising "guests" of the hotel made, and when they reached for their trousers to dress themselves, they not only found that these had disappeared, but that their shoes, hats and what proved to be their heaviest loss, their coats in which they had their purses with every cent that they possessed, had taken wing during the night from beneath their pillows, where they had hidden them for safety. They tried to explain their loss to the other inmates, but instead of receiving sympathy for their trouble, only malicious grunts and malevolent leers were their reward.

'Let's Get out of This Horrid Place,' Whispered Jim, when by the Unsteady Yellow Light of the Candle He Counted Five Bunks, one Above the Other, Each of Which Held a Sleeping Hobo.

A few moments later the manager, having been apprised of the theft, entered the dimly lighted quarters, not to search the other bunks for their stolen property, but merely to console his robbed guests, so they would not report their loss to the police and cause unpleasant comment in the papers. While they listened to him they saw only ugly scowls upon the rum-soaked visages of the other inmates of the place, who had crowded around and seemed to greatly enjoy their misfortune, and who broke into shouts of boisterous laughter when the manager explained to the boys that the golden rule of the "Golden Rule Hotel" had always read: "Do everybody—before they do you."

CHAPTER VII.
"False Friends."

The manager of the "Golden Rule Hotel" raked up a couple of outfits of cast-off hobo clothing, and coaxed Joe and Jim into dressing themselves into these, and then advised the twins to quickly find employment so they could purchase better attire.

On the preceding day, when they were yet the possessors of almost fifty dollars, they had refused many offers of good employment, but now when they made the rounds calling upon the same employers, dressed as they were in their tattered clothes, to plead for a chance to be permitted to earn a living, these same men had suddenly become stony-hearted and some of them even refused to listen to their tale of how their clothes had been stolen from them. They attempted to fill jobs at common labor, but even in this they did not succeed, as their young bodies lacked the necessary strength to wield the heavy picks and shovels.

When the dinner hour arrived, Jim, who had never been in all his life as hungry as he was at this moment, remarked that he thought it would be best to hobo the next train back to their home, but Joe caused him to quickly get over this attack of homesickness, when he asked if Jim had the nerve to dare face their mother without a cent and in the rags he wore.

When the street lamps were lighted and the stores and offices commenced to be closed for the night, they made their way back to the "Golden Rule Hotel" where, luckily for them, they had at least a place to sleep in the bunks for which they had settled a week in advance.

While they walked down the city's thoroughfares, they were attracted by the splendor and the brilliant illumination of a restaurant. They stopped and with famished countenances looked through the French plate glass windows and watched the diners enjoy toothsome tidbits, and then wearily moved on—their pride would not permit them to wait for a departing diner to accost him for the price of a loaf of bread wherewith to still their gnawing hunger.

When they entered the "Golden Rule Hotel" office not a single word of greeting or sympathy was extended to them; on the contrary, the manager cautioned them to be careful not to have their present suits stolen from them during the night, and they realized how true was the perverted meaning he had given to the Golden Rule.

It was yet early in the evening and none of the other inmates had retired for the night, but so completely exhausted were the boys that they asked for a candle and then in the semi-darkness of the hall found the numbers of the bunks they had occupied the preceding nights. Remembering the manager's warning to take better care of their property, they placed their clothes under the straw stuffed mattresses.

*They Stopped in Front of a Brilliantly Illuminated Restaurant and
Watched With Famished Countenances Diners Enjoy Toothsome Dainties.*

They blew out the candle, but just at the moment when they were ready to crawl into their bunks, Jim whispered to Joe: "Brother, come let us pray the way, mother has taught us." And there in the darkness of the hall they knelt upon the bare floor, and while their torturing consciences told them that their own misfortunes were only a fraction of the woe they themselves had inflicted upon their poor, widowed mother, they pleaded with God to assist them in the extremity of their distress and at least not permit them to perish of sheer starvation.

At break-of-day, aroused from a fitful sleep by the gnawing of their hunger, they dragged themselves down to the hotel office to scan the morning papers for some chance to find employment. But even this early there were several fellows ahead of them eagerly copying addresses from the want columns. While they waited for their turn to look into the paper, several lodgers came down stairs. "Are you looking for jobs, my lads?" they were addressed in a friendly manner by one of these early-risers, who was a rather small fellow and whose clothes and general appearance were somewhat above the average of the other inmates of the hotel, and as the twins nodded assent to his query, he continued: "Are you strangers in Minneapolis?" And as Joe affirmed this question he in a still more friendly tone added: "It's a hard matter for strangers, expecially if they are not dressed in style, to find employment in this city at this time of the year." His confiding conversation so impressed the thoroughly disheartened twins that upon his further questioning, they recounted to him their experiences since the moment they climbed into the empty box car that brought them to Minneapolis.

The fellow listened attentively to their story of misfortune and then asked them to give to him their correct name and home address. Joe, thinking that at last they had found a sympathizing friend, cheerfully furnished the stranger with their correct names, and gave to him as the address of their home the name of their lone prairie siding, Rugby, North Dakota. Then their newly made acquaintance pulled out a notebook into which he carefully wrote their addresses. Next he proposed that they wait for the appearance of his pal, who was yet on the floor above them, when all of them would go out and eat breakfast.

"A man's stomach is his best friend", and no sooner had the fellow invited the starving lads, who for more than thirly-six hours had not tasted a solid bite, than they overwhelmed their friend with proofs of their gratitude.

A little later their benefactor's partner, a medium-sized, clean shaven and neatly attired fellow, came down the stairway. Their friend called him aside and they held a hurried conversation. Then they joined the twins and all went to a nearby restaurant. While the lads made away with a quantity of food that caused the astonished waiter to gape with surprise, their two benefactors, while they rattled silver dollars in their pockets, explained to the lads that Chicago was a far better city for them to find employment in than either Minneapolis or St.

Paul, and that if the twins would join them on a hobo trip to that city they would see to it that they would not suffer until a job was found for them.

It was just like hanging candy before a baby, and Joe and Jim without a second thought accepted their offer. After they had settled for their breakfasts, they took the agreeably surprised youngsters into a clothing store and bought for each of them a serviceable outfit of clothes, and it now was not a matter if the boys would go with the strangers, but if the strangers would accept the boys, soul and body.

"I propose that we get out of Minneapolis as quickly as we can," suggested the fellow whom they first met in the "Golden Rule Hotel" office, and his pal assented and they walked to the railroad station where they purchased tickets to the first station beyond St. Paul and within an hour they were aboard a train traveling to their new destination.

Upon their arrival at this station, a small hamlet, their first acquaintance told them that his road name was "Kansas Shorty" and his partner's "Slippery". The lads were surprised that these men should not use their Christian names, but as they were accustomed to hearing all the section laborers and every harvester called by a "monicker" or "name-de-rail", they kept their thoughts to themselves, and Joe, after listening to these instructions gleefully remarked: "Gee, I wish that you would give each of us a hobo name the same as you have." After some discussion they nicknamed Joe, "Dakota Joe" and Jim, "Dakota Jim."

They waited for some time to try to hobo some passing train, but as none of them stopped or slowed up sufficiently for them to risk swinging onto it, when the dinner hour drew near, Slippery visited a nearby country store and soon returned carrying canned foods and other material from which they could prepare a substantial "Mulligan", which is made by stewing in a large tin can almost everything edible over a slow fire. They collected some castaway tin cans and then went to a thicket by the side of a rippling brook, where they built a roaring fire and when the embers began to form they placed upon the glowing coals the tin can containing the "mulligan".

Then all repaired to the side of the brook to scour the cans and make their own dinner toilets, and here, while the twins washed their faces, their pals noticed for the first time the singular white hair-growths upon the backs of their heads, their inheritance from their forefathers. Joe explained to their wondering companions that these streaks of white hair were their birth-marks, but Slippery, afraid that these conspicuous freaks of nature would draw too much attention to their young comrades, collected some sprigs of sage, and after he had pounded the same to a pulp between some stones, rubbed it into the white hair upon the boy's heads, with the result that within a few moments they were dyed to almost the same shade as the rest of their scalps.

By this time the "mulligan" was ready to serve and they dined upon the savory hobo-stew, and after they had filled their inner selves, according to hobo usage they stretched themselves in the shade of the trees to take their after-dinner rest. Unused to the ways of the road, yet pleased with the fate that had brought them into the partnership of men who at least provided them with substantial meals, soon the satisfied snores that emanated from their throats proved to the others that the twins had landed in dreamland.

The moment Kansas Shorty, who had anxiously waited for this chance, had assured himself that the lads were soundly sleeping, he beckoned to his pal and both moved beyond the earshot of the sleepers. "Slippery," Kansas Shorty addressed his pal, "what do you think of our lucky catch in the 'Road Kid Line'? Don't you think that we are the luckiest tramps that ever rambled over any railroad to make a catch of two healthy and good-looking lads as these two are?" And then after he had permitted his cunning eyes to wander back over the forms of the peacefully sleeping lads he continued: "And wasn't it funny to see how they appreciated the breakfasts we bought for them, the new store suits we paid for, and how eagerly they accepted our offer to permit them to hobo with us to Chicago, and how now they are blindly devoted to us, willing to follow us through Hades?" Here Kansas Shorty paused and added in a whisper, "And wouldn't they be surprised if they knew the truth, that they had paid for their own as well as our meals, their new suits, their railroad tickets, and even the mulligan with their own money, as we are the ones who, during the darkness of the night robbed their bunks at the Golden Rule Hotel?" Then the two rascals broke into hearty laughter, as they recalled how, amongst the hundreds of the homeless wretches who lodged at the Golden Rule Hotel, they were the ones guilty of having stolen everything the twins possessed in the world, and when Kansas Shorty repeated: "First we stole their clothes, then we found their well-filled purses, and now, to finish our streak of luck we have them thrown into the bargain," they renewed their laughter, which was abruptly stopped when Kansas Shorty suddenly asked his pal what he intended to do with the lads. "Of course we can take them to Chicago with us and find them some sort of a job, and thus rid ourselves of their presence," answered Slippery, intending to shed himself of their useless company, and ever wary of trouble he wisely added, "Kansas Shorty, you well know the trite saying: 'Two is company; three is a crowd; four is the road to disaster,' so let us give the lads a square deal and take them with us to Chicago and 'drop' them there after finding employment for them." But hardly had he finished this well-meant suggestion, than Kansas Shorty almost in a rage retorted: "Slippery, you are proving yourself to be a regular yegg by the soft talk you have just been giving me. You belong to the class of men who steal and rob, while I am a "plinger", and beg for a living. To your kind a boy is a handicap, while to our class a good-looking boy is a most decided asset as a boy to us means a heavy increase of our incomes and of our comforts, and now you tell me that you are anxious to find jobs for these lads whom I could easily train into first-class Road Kids." Slippery, dumfounded at the almost monstrous proposition his comrade made, who was ready and willing to spoil the youngsters' futures by transforming them into common beggars, failed to find an immediate answer, and now Kansas Shorty, abusively speaking, continued: "You, Slippery, have been my rambling-male for almost a month, but now I propose that we part comradeship and you travel on to Chicago and let me take charge of these sleeping lads, as I do not wish other plingers to know that I have been guilty enough to permit two likely looking lads to slip through my hands by permitting them to accept employment, and" he added as a sort of final argument, "when I take charge of these kids, I shall know how to keep my bread well buttered."

Although Slippery himself was a confirmed criminal, he bore only the deepest of loathing for that class of scoundrels of which Kansas Shorty had proudly proclaimed himself a member, and his hatred of the begging class of tramps welled up in him and with a sudden movement his hand swung back to his hip pocket and glaring in a most menacing manner at Kansas Shorty he waited for further developments. Seeing that Slippery meant business, this scoundrel now took recourse in diplomacy. "Slippery, old pal," the miserable coward stammered, while at the same time his eyes followed the yegg's arm down to where he saw his hand gripping a large caliber revolver, and although perceiving his danger should he further provoke the anger of his pal, he was unwilling to give up the youngsters without at least a struggle, "what is the use of two such chums as we have been until this moment, to quarrel about a couple of good-for-nothing runaway kids? Let me make you a fair proposition. You said that two is company, while three is a crowd, and as I am sure you will not court the risk to drag two road kids with you past all the Johnny Laws (policemen) who will get wise to you when you have a "family" hoboing with you, I propose that you take one of these lads with you to Chicago, while I shall take it upon me to look after the other one," and when he noted that Slippery's hand had loosened its grip from the pistol, he said in almost pleading tones, "two of them will be entirely too many for you, while one will make a good companion for you in yegging, and the other one will make a good assistant for me in plinging, and to promptly settle the question whom each one is to take let's flip a dollar into the air, and if it falls with the head up you take your choice, while if the eagle turns up I have the first pick."

Slippery gave in to Kansas Shorty's plausible argument because he not only wished to avoid bloodshed, but he also realized that the two lads would be a handicap to him, as he had his face and Bertillon measurements in every rogue's gallery in the country, and he saw a chance to thus peaceably rid himself of his companion, whom he now despised far more than he would a rattlesnake.

He gave a nod with his head and Kansas Shorty flipped the dollar high into the air, and when it fell to the ground the eagle showed up on top, and Kansas Shorty went over to Jim, who seemed to him somewhat more tractable then his brother Joe, and more suited for his purposes. He awakened him and then aroused Joe, and explained to both that instead of rambling directly to Chicago, while they had been sleeping, Slippery and he had decided to tackle for employment the many farms which they saw on both sides of the railroad track, and that Joe should accompany Slippery, while Jim had been selected by him as his companion in this job-hunting venture. The unsuspecting lads readily assented to this fair sounding proposition, the more as Kansas Shorty, although he cautioned Slippery to meet him and Jim that evening under the "big oak", never exchanged another word with his partner.

"So long, until tonight," called Jim to Joe, who returned his brother's farewell, and soon Kansas Shorty with Jim by his side was walking northward upon the railroad track, until around a curve, which placed them out of view of the other pair, who were walking upon the track southward, he left the right-of-way at a road crossing and struck westward upon a public highway into the interior.

The flip of the coin had decided their fate. It meant for James McDonald that he had become an apprentice to Kansas Shorty, the Plinger—a begging tramp; while for Joseph McDonald it spelled that he had become a companion to Slippery, the Yegg—a criminal tramp.

CHAPTER VIII.
"Busting a Broncho."

For three long days after they had parted company with the others, Kansas Shorty kept Jim aimlessly wandering with him about the country, carefully avoiding the railroads, as he did not wish to meet other tramps while Jim was yet "green" to the dark ways of the road, as they by wily tricks and methods often entice new road kids from their partners, who in the language of the road are known as "jockers".

From the moment that Kansas Shorty had Jim out of the view of Slippery and Joe, he commenced training the lad into the infamous ways of the road, so as to properly prepare him for his future work. The first and most important lesson he gave the unsuspecting youngster consisted in poisoning his faith in humanity by teaching him that henceforth he must consider and treat every human being, except his pal, as his bitter enemy. To prove that to be a fact he would call the lad's attention to the suspicious looks everybody whom they passed upon the public highway would cast at them. The second lesson was to impress upon Jim the importance of never revealing his correct name and address to any inquisitive questioner, but to always take refuge behind some common name such as Jones, Brown or Smith, and to give some faraway city as his place of residence. He taught the boy many other vicious tricks, and to prevent suspicions arising in the lad's mind that everything was not on the square, Kansas Shorty would let him wait for him in the public highway, after he had told him that he would call at a nearby farm house and try to find jobs for both. He would then knock on the farm house door, and if someone answered his knocks would ask for a match, a pin or some other trifle and then return to the waiting lad and bitterly complain about his inability to find employment.

Towards the evening of the first day, Jim becoming somewhat anxious to meet his brother, and observing that Kansas Shorty made not the slightest move to reach the "big oak", which he had told Slippery should be their meeting place, he casually remarked: "Say, friend, is it not close to the time that we should find our way to the "big oak" where we are to meet Slippery and my brother Joe?" "It's plenty time until then," was Kansas Shorty's reply, and then to show Jim that he was from now on his master, he angrily added: "You do not need to remind me again, as I shall take care of you."

Just as dusk blended into the night, after they had supped upon a handout that he had begged at a farm house, Kansas Shorty pointed his hand in the direction of some oaks which were growing some distance from the highway and told Jim that beneath the tallest of them was the place where they were to meet Slippery and Joe.

They climbed over fences and crossed fields, and the closer they approached the tree the more Jim's heart palpitated, so anxious was he to rejoin his twin brother, whose inseparable companion he had been since their birth until this day, and strange forebodings seemed to have told him that all was not well, as Kansas Shorty during their conversation had contradicted himself in many statements, and too, they had passed farm house after farm house and many people in the public highway during the last two hours without his trying to apply to them for a job.

When they reached the oak and Jim found that neither Slippery nor Joe had put in an appearance, he began to lament, and when Kansas Shorty assured him that he could only account for their absence by believing they had been jailed on a "suspicious character" charge, the frightened lad commenced to sob.

Kansas Shorty feeling in need of a night's rest, climbed across fences into a nearby field and gathered some new-mown hay from which he fashioned beneath the protecting branches of the oak a comfortable resting place for himself and Jim. But before he went to sleep, to prevent Jim from taking French leave, he induced the boy to take off his shoes and his coat out of which he made for himself a pillow, and after he had assured the lad that Slippery and Joe would certainly find them should they arrive during the night, he turned over on to his side and was soon soundly sleeping.

On the morning of the fourth day they struck a railroad for the first time since they left it. It proved to be the St. Paul-Omaha main line of the Chicago and Northwestern System, and as luck would have it, while they were walking up a steep grade a stock train loaded with sheep passed them so slowly that they found it an easy matter to swing themselves onto it and they climbed through an open end-door into one of the stock cars, in which, hidden amongst the sheep, they managed to hobo unmolested through many division points where they bought provisions while the sheep were being fed and watered. On the morning of the third day they landed, not at Chicago, as Kansas Shorty had until now made Jim believe, but at Denver, the beautiful capital city of Colorado.

While they walked about the streets of the city, Kansas Shorty met a friend whom he addressed as "Nevada Bill," and who as soon as the former told him that Jim was "his road kid", placed his hand under the boy's chin and after sizing the lad up just as a butcher would a beef, he whispered: "Well, well, Kansas Shorty, I see you have brought a fine 'broncho' to town with you. I hope that you will be able to make a first-class road kid of him." To which coarse remarks Kansas Shorty laughingly replied: "Never fret, Nevada Bill, I have trained many a road kid into good plingers." Nevada Bill then told him where a gang of plingers had their headquarters, and as Kansas Shorty seemed to be acquainted with most of them whose monickers Nevada Bill repeated to him, he decided to pay this gang a visit.

They wended their way through Denver's lowest slums and finally arrived at the headquarters of this gang of professional tramp beggars, who always prefer cities in which to ply their trade, and only strike out to visit smaller places and the country at large—and then only in separate pairs—when too many of them drifted into the same city, so as to make combing the public for money an unprofitable business, or when the police made a general raid upon vagrants of their class.

This last reason was hardly to be feared, for as in this gang's case, they invariably have their headquarters in the building above a slum saloon, whose proprietor would and could not be in business very long unless he knew how to protect his lodgers against police interference, as a gang's quarters needed to be raided only one time, and ever after all plingers in the land would give this unsafe "dump," as tramps call this class of hangout, a wide berth, as this raid sufficiently proved to them that this slum saloon was not properly "protected."

Up the well-worn stairway they climbed and when they reached the second floor of the building Kansas Shorty knocked on a door, which was only opened to them after he had given an account of his identity, and when they entered the room, that by another open door was connected with an adjoining second one, Jim, to his complete surprise found himself in the company of eight grown, burly hoboes of the roughest imaginable type and almost a school class of road kids.

Kansas Shorty was most cordially welcomed by the men occupying the rooms, who insisted that he and his road kid should make their home with them during their stay in Denver, which offer he gladly accepted. Then he introduced Jim as "Dakota Jim" to the others and made the lad shake hands with each and everyone of the ragged, filthy and foul-visaged fellows, who, as Kansas Shorty had told Jim upon the street before he had found their hiding place, were "proper" tramps and explained to him that this meant that all of them were recognized amongst their own kind as worthy members of the fraternity.

After he had shaken hands with the ugly, rum-bloated specimens of humanity, Jim had a chance to take a look at the two rooms which were to be his future home, and his thoughts went back to his mother's cleanly kept section house, for the total of the furniture in these rooms consisted of some empty soap boxes which served for chairs, a slime-covered table, a couple of rough wooden benches, a piece of mirror glass that was upheld by nails driven into the bare walls, a range, upon which at this moment a dinner was cooking, and two dilapidated beds, the pillows, blankets and mattresses of which—there was no trace of linen—were in an even far more filthy condition than the bunks of the "Golden Rule Hotel" at Minneapolis.

Jim was aroused from his survey of the rooms by Kansas Shorty, who now introduced him to each one of the road kids, whose jockers called aloud the name-de-road of each.

Some of these jockers had as many as four of these lads, whose ages ranged from ten to twenty years, and whose sizes were from that of mere children to fellows who shaved themselves daily so as to pass muster as "road kids". To have seen these road kids one would have never imagined that within the course of a few short years every one of these boys would be transformed into the same class of sodden wretches their jockers now were, who had trained them into the ways of the road, and that they in turn during their life time would spoil the futures of scores of sons of respectable parents, which proves that degeneration breeds degeneration.

One of the road kids in the den of the plingers, who was known by the name of "Danny" because of his neat appearance and superior intelligence, attracted Jim's attention and gave a fair average example of the parentage of the rest. When after their short acquaintance in a burst of confidence Jim acquainted Danny with the fact that his late father had been the foreman and commander of a section crew of a North Dakota railroad, Danny puckered up his lips in utter contempt when he informed and proved to the surprised Jim that he was the son of a wealthy banker of Fort Worth, Texas, and—another proof of boyish thoughtlessness—had skipped school to hop freight trains in the railroad yards of his home city. One day he had watched some wandering hoboes cooking a mulligan by a campfire, and had helped to eat the stew, and through this had made the first acquaintance of his present jocker, who had enticed the little lad to run away from his home and follow him out on the road; had trained him into making a living for both; had taught him first to drink, then to like and last to crave strong liquor, and although he treated the lad as a master would his slave, he gave him daily a regular allowance of diluted alcohol, which caused his young victim to quickly forget all desire to return to his home and his parents as there he could not secure the dram he yearned.

Their conversation was interrupted by one of the grown hoboes, who, acting as cook, called all hands to "dinner". This dinner, which was another mulligan, was placed in the center of the table in the same pot in which it had been cooked, and each member of the gang, just as if they were still camping about a hobo fire in the woods, by means of a small wooden paddle pulled as much of the mulligan as he desired, onto a tin plate, that had never been touched by dishwater, but had only been scraped since the day it arrived at the rooms.

During their meal, also before they commenced to dine and after they had finished, in fact all the time except when they were sleeping, a "human chain" was kept busy fetching from the slum saloon on the ground floor of the building a steady stream of "growlers" filled with beer and diluted, sweetened alcohol, which passed as "whiskey", and returning the empty tin cans for further supplies, as not the small rent of the rooms but the large and steady thirst of their inmates made it very profitable for the dive keepers to lodge this class of human perverts.

Kansas Shorty Pulled the Lad Across the Table, and After one of the inhuman Monsters Had Stuffed a Filthy Rag into the Poor Boy's Mouth to Smother His Pitiful Screams, they Pounded Him Until He Became Unconscious.

After they had finished their dinner the two filth-laden beds, the benches, the table and even the slime covered floor became sleeping places for the satiated tramps and their road kids, and gradually as their cigarettes burned low and their coarse conversation lagged, all of them, greatly assisted by the strong drink they had swallowed, dozed away.

All of them—with the exception of James McDonald, who had not yet sunken to the sodden level of these brutes in human forms who lay scattered about the two rooms, dead to the world in maudlin sleep, proving themselves to be living models of every stage of the decaying influences of hobo life, from men whose countenances had been turned into bloated visages down to the pale faces of the younger boys who had just commenced to feel the curse of the lives which they had been forced by these jockers to lead.

While Jim sat amongst them upon an empty upturned soap box, his eyes wandered from one to the other of these wretched beings, who from this time on would be his pals and companions and whose lives gave him a vivid picture of what his own future would be. Suddenly the blood welled up in him, and although he knew that hundreds of miles of unknown country separated him from his home and mother, one desire outbalanced everything, that was the wish to escape the fate of these hoboes and the longer he looked at the alcohol disfigured masks of these human vultures who, too, had once been clean and manly lads, the more fierce became his resolve to now or never escape the clutches of Kansas Shorty, who was sleeping as heavily as the others.

He scanned again the face of each one of the hoboes, and especially that of Kansas Shorty, and after he had assured himself that all were soundly sleeping he carefully stepped over the bodies of those who lay between him and his liberty—the door that led into the hallway—but as he turned its knob, which being rusty from age and filth, creaked considerably, its grating noise awakened one of the road kids, who fathoming the reason of Jim's opening the door and darting into the hallway, let out a piercing shout, "that Kansas Shorty's kid was making his get-away". This warning shriek not only awakened every one of the sleepers but sobered Kansas Shorty so suddenly that he made a headlong dive through the open door, beyond which Jim was running down the hallway trying to make his escape. He caught the lad before he even reached the stairway and dragged the shuddering boy back into the filthy room, carefully locking the door behind them.

He pulled the boy across the table, and after one of the inhuman monsters had stuffed a filthy rag into the poor lad's mouth to smother his screams, Kansas Shorty, as the jocker of the lad, gleefully assisted by the others in his savage task, pounded poor Jim until he became unconscious.

When Jim came to, Kansas Shorty, of whom he expected this last of all, was sitting upon the edge of the bed upon which he had been placed, and while he fanned the poor boy's bruised and battered face with a folded newspaper, he was talking to him in a softly purring voice, telling him how sorry he felt to have been forced to punish him for having attempted to run away from his "protector", who intended to make out of "Dakota Jim" a "man" who in the future would be proud to tell other plingers that Kansas Shorty had been his jocker.

Kansas Shorty continued to speak in this petting and almost flattering vein, while at the same time he fed the feverish and maltreated lad with pieces of choice candy and other tidbits for which he had sent while Jim was yet unconscious, and stroked the boy's hair and dressed his wounds with vaseline-soaked rags and showed in every possible manner how true a friend he was to Jim, to whom he repeated over and over the fact that he had clothed and fed him in Minneapolis when he and his brother Joe were on the verge of death by starvation. He never stopped his flow of pleasing language, ever harping upon the good he had done and would do for Jim, if the latter would only trust him, until forced by sheer friendless loneliness the boy folded his bruised arms around Kansas Shorty's neck and amid heart-broken sobs begged his pardon for having tried to leave him, and while the other hoboes in the room, old as well as young, who had all passed through the same sort of treatment, had a hard time to suppress their smiles, he solemnly promised to never again attempt to escape.

Then the poor boy sank back upon the bed and gradually, urged on by Kansas Shorty's assurance that sleep would heal all the quicker the bruises and marks the terrible beating had left on him, a reminder of his promise, and a warning of far worse punishment should he dare to break it, he fell asleep.

Then the other plingers sent down to the slum saloon for a new supply of beer and "whiskey", and while they took care not to make noise enough to awaken the new recruit to the army of professional beggars, they drank to Kansas Shorty's health and congratulated him upon the successful culmination of the first step necessary to make a good-for-nothing parasite of society out of a respectable boy. This inhuman brutality is administered to every boy who falls into the clutches of a plinger, as it not only deadens the spirit of pride and honor, but makes the boy obedient to the least command of his jocker.

This cruel maltreatment is called amongst those hoboes who have boys tramping with them: "Busting a Broncho".

CHAPTER IX.
"The Abyss."

The following law, if passed and enforced without mercy, would quickly put a stop to the common practice of degenerates spoiling the lives and futures of other people's children by training them to become tramps, drunkards, professional beggars and even dangerous criminals, viz: "Should any minor be found beyond the limits of his legal residence tramping, peddling, begging or stealing at the command or for the benefit of an adult person, who cannot prove that he had the legal consent of the minor's guardian, then this adult person shall be sentenced to a long term at hard labor in the state penitentiary."

(The actual experiences of the Author, who when a young boy was at one time a plinger's road kid, are embodied into this chapter and have been even far more revolting than herein described.)

It was several days after the terrible thrashing before Jim recovered sufficiently to be able to show himself upon the streets.

On the morning of the fifth day after his arrival at Denver, he was told by Kansas Shorty to accompany Danny upon his day's work and watch how this small, weak boy managed to earn a living for himself and his master, who under the pretense of "showing him the world", had enticed him away from his home.

Danny had been trained by his jocker, an ugly ex-convict, who on account of his ape-like face had been dubbed "Jocko", to peddle needle cases from house to house. These needle cases are paper packages containing an assortment of needles and are always retailed in every store in the land for five cents. These harmless packages have made more useless, if not dangerous men out of harmless youngsters than any other cause, as printed in bold type across their face are these words:

"PRICE 25 CENTS".

This fictitious price mark works straight into the hands of the jockers who purchase these needle cases by the gross for about two cents each and teach their road kids to dispose of them, at a huge profit. If needle cases can not be had, sticking plaster, aluminum thimbles, pencils, shoestrings and other such articles are given to the road kids to peddle.

From the pages of a Denver City Directory, Jocko had copied upon sheets of paper the name, street and house number of every resident in the city, overlooking none, as sometimes those who occupy humble homes buy more needle cases and turn out more revenue than those who reside in marble palaces.

Jocko had handed Danny a list of names and addresses and the road kid's trick, which his ugly jocker had most carefully rehearsed with him, was worked by calling at residences and by correctly quoting the names foil the servants and obtain an interview with the lady of the house to whom he would tell a story that would make a "stone weep." With Jim by his side this morning he spoke of him as being his cousin, and with a string of woeful lies attached to his yarn he usually managed not only to receive the price printed upon the package, which he held up in such a position that the lady could not fail to see its fictitious value, but oftentimes he received more than this sum.

They sold a number of the needle cases, and although Jim had a look of complete disgust upon his face, showing how he disapproved of Danny's lying, the latter, proud as a peacock, instead of being ashamed of swindling kind-hearted ladies, said in a tone of voice which left no doubt that he would do exactly as he proposed: "Eh, Jim, when I get to be a plinger I shall have at least a dozen road kids peddling for me and not like Jocko, who besides myself has only three other kids hustling for him," and after a pause he disdainfully added, just as if his jocker was not already doing incalculable harm, "only four kids, with so many of them hoboing about the country."

At one of the houses, after Danny had repeated his tale of woe, a charitable lady told them to await her return as she had left her purse in her bed room, located on the second floor. Never suspecting that boys appealing for assistance would turn into ingrates, she left the front door ajar. The next moment Jim almost sank to the floor when he saw Danny sneak into the house, enter the nearest room, and just as the lady descended the stairs, dart back to his former place upon the porch, holding a silver spoon in his hand, which he hid in his pocket. After the lady had paid him for a needle case they left.

Danny repeated this disgraceful trick of basest ingratitude at several other houses. Then he coaxed Jim into making the lying appeal necessary to sell the needle cases, and whenever Jim managed to make a sale Danny's praises knew no bounds. Finally Danny had just one needle case left out of the stock Jocko had handed to him to peddle, and while they waited before the open entrance door of a palatial residence for the return of the lady of the house, who had left them to find her pocketbook, and whose footfalls they could hear as she descended the stairway leading into the basement of her home, Danny deliberately pushed the unsuspecting Jim through the half-open door into the hall of the mansion, and told him in a whisper that if he did not steal something he "would tell Kansas Shorty."

In all his past life Jim had never stolen a single cent's worth of other people's property, but with Danny threatening to tell Kansas Shorty should he refuse to do as told, and remembering the cruel pounding he had received at the hands of this fiend only such a short time before, and the warning ere he and Danny set out upon their begging trip to do exactly as Danny ordered, he realized that perhaps another far more brutal beating would be his should he disobey Danny's command.

Before him was an open door, and when he entered the room he found it to be the parlor. Looking about he saw a glittering gold watch lying upon the piano, and picked it up, and gazed at it for a moment. "No, I must not disgrace my honest name by becoming a common thief for the mere sake of furnishing sodden wretches with rum," he mused, but while he hesitated he heard the footfalls of the lady of the house as she ascended the stairs, then the fear of the terrible punishment that would be his if he disobeyed conquered his honesty and he slipped the time piece into his pocket and joined Danny at the entrance.

When the lady of the house came to the door she handed Danny a bright silver dollar and when he wanted to give her the needle case she refused to take it from him, and while tears of pity streamed down her face she said: "May God forbid that I take from you poor unfortunate boys an article that you could dispose of to others, and thus further assist your starving parents", and before the lads could utter a sound she had shut the door in their faces.

It was now half past eleven in the morning, and as road kids do "housework" only between nine and this time of the day, as after these hours the police commence to be more active and the ladies become far less inclined to listen to a tale of distress, they went back to the plinger's headquarters.

In strict accordance with the unwritten code of the road although Jocko, his ugly-visaged jocker, was amongst those in the room, Danny paid not the least attention to his presence, but stepped up to the table upon which an empty tin plate had been placed for just this purpose, and deposited upon it every cent he had in his pockets and whatever he had pilfered from the houses.

Danny now told Jim to place the watch he had stolen upon the tin plate, which he did. Kansas Shorty picked it up and estimated its value at not less than one hundred dollars, and then praised Jim for having upon his first raid proven himself to be a first-class road kid, and that the "gang" was proud to call him a pal. When Jim was out of hearing Danny received much praise for having turned an honest boy into a beggar and a thief by the same methods that he had been taught by his jocker and other road kids.

So quickly had these rum-soaked, heartless monsters converted an absolutely harmless lad into a criminal, that Jim pleaded with Kansas Shorty to permit him to try unassisted to peddle needle cases. He was not accorded this privilege, but was sent out with a boy nicknamed "Snippy". This boy had a most repulsive looking sore upon his arm, reaching from the wrist four inches upward. His graft consisted of visiting offices located in the business district and showing to persons this noisome sore, and then handing them the begging letter his jocker had faked for him, he collected alms, while at the same time he contorted his face as if suffering agony from his "disease".

After Supper Jim Watched a Hobo Paint Acid into the Dreadful Sore upon Snippy's Arm and Heard the Little Lad Shriek With Pain when the Fluid ate into His Quivering Flesh.

When they returned to the hangout at the end of his working hours at 2 p.m., as the afternoon mails made charity calls of this class unprofitable, Jim was given his third lesson by a lad who went by the hobo name of "Spanish John."

On the preceding evening John and Jim had played catch ball in the hallway and the way John chased after a ball he had failed to catch caused Jim to greatly admire the boy's agility.

But this morning John certainly looked for all the world as if he had passed through a long war. He upheld his body by means of a pair of crutches and his face was all furrowed as if he were suffering agony, while his left foot was drawn high above the ground just as if a cannon ball had made its acquaintance, and it was with such a sad voice that he called to Jim to follow him, that Jim felt so sorry for John he forgot to ask him what had happened to him since both chased the elusive ball in the hallway.

Spanish John had a sore upon his left leg just like Snippy had upon his arm, and he used this sore, assisted by small cards called "duckets", upon which an "appeal" was printed, to swindle honest and well meaning people out of money. Proprietors of stores and shops were his favorites. When supper time approached and while upon their way back to the plingers' quarters, after they had left the business section, John handed his crutches to Jim to carry, and told the astounded lad, who supposed John had actually been crippled, that limping with crutches was a "most tiresome job."

Everyone of the road kids had been trained by his jocker to become a specialist in some particular brand of the begging game. One of them had around his arm a plaster of Paris casting, that during his begging trips would be filled with cotton upon which a few drops of carbolic acid or some other "medicinally" smelling liquid had been poured, to give the "phoney" broken-arm trick a cloak of respectability. When not at "work" the "dummy" was shoved far above the boy's elbow and tied so that it did not interfere with his playing "tag", and other boyish games.

A simple-faced chap, but one who knew the game from A to Z, played the deaf and dumb game, for which purpose his jocker had forced him to learn the sign language. Another boy had been taught to throw his hand and fingers so far "out of joint" that a real crippled-for-life paralytic could not have improved upon the deceptive deformity. Both of these lads used duckets, pencils, shoestrings and thimbles as an addition to their mute appeals, although it is a well-known fact that no genuinely afflicted paralytics or mutes, least of all boys, ever resort to begging for their living.

In the evening after supper had been served and things had somewhat quieted down in the rooms, almost dumfounded by surprise Jim watched Snippy's jocker paint a strong solution of lye into the dreadful sore—known in the hobo vernacular as a "jigger"—upon the road kid's arm. The poor little lad shrieked with pain as the acid ate into his quivering flesh, which deepened the wound

still more and gave it a "fresh" look, which greatly added to its horrid repulsive-
ness so as to all the more arouse the pity of those from whom he would be
forced to beg on the coming morning.

Joe made careful inquiries of one of the friends he had made among the road
kids, and this boy told him that oftentimes these inhuman monsters continued
the lye treatment for such a length of time and so fearfully corroded their helpless victim's limbs, that blood-poisoning set in and made amputations necessary
to save their lives. The deeply seared, white scars which these "jiggers" leave
during the balance of the road kids' natural lives, prove to those who are versed
in the ways of the road, in which school of crime a criminal branded with these
tell-tale scars received his first lesson.

Just before Jim went to rest for the night upon one of the bare wooden benches
that had been given to him for his bed, Kansas Shorty warned him that if he
ever said a single word of what had occurred since he left Minneapolis, or
would occur in the future, he would not only murder him but would ramble to
Rugby and tell his mother that her son had robbed a house, and then he pulled
out his notebook and repeated to Jim his correct name and address, which the
boy had in his innocence given him at the Golden Rule Hotel.

The poor lad first shuddered with terror as he thought how his poor mother
would suffer should she be informed how he had disgraced her, then he snuggled close to the black-souled fiend and solemnly promised never to divulge a
single word to any mortal.

The following morning Kansas Shorty gave Jim a package of needle cases and
in words that Jim could not misunderstand ordered him not to come "home" until every one had been peddled.

Luck was with him. His rosy cheeks and his neat appearance opened the hearts
and loosened the purse strings of charitable ladies and it was just ten o'clock
when he returned to the hangout, having sold all of his stock.

Jim pleaded to be permitted at least until the noon hour to sell more needle
cases, and his jocker, pleased to see the the lad so anxious to support an able-
bodied hobo loafer in idleness, consented and gave him another supply.

Again fortune favored him and when a nearby clock pointed its hands to a
quarter of twelve he had just one needle case left. He rang the door bell of a residence, and as if luck was with him, the lady of the house, a matron with snowy
hair and features which in every line bespoke the kind-heartness of her soul,
opened the door. After he had explained to her his errand, she took the needle
case out of his hand and then told him to await her return as she had left her
pocket book in her bed room upon the second floor of her home. She went,
leaving the front door ajar.

Jim heard the lady of the house mount the stairway, then the second flight, now
she was walking towards the rear of the building, and when he heard a door

slam, indicating that she had entered the bed room, like a flash of lightning an evil thought shot through his mind. It was just one step to the open parlor door. He craned his head, and looked into the parlor, and when he saw that the shades were drawn, which would prevent his being seen from the outside, he thought that this would be a fine chance to show to Kansas Shorty, Danny and all the rest of his "friends" how well he had learned their lessons.

Without the least hesitation he stepped into the semi-darkness of the parlor, where his eyes were attracted by the gleaming steel of a large caliber revolver lying upon the center table. He heard the lady's footfalls as she descended from the second flight of stairs, and quickly reaching out his hand he picked up the pistol and slipped it into his pocket. He then turned about, to quietly take his former place before the front door, but just as he turned, he felt a pair of hands grip him from behind by the throat. He struggled hard to free himself from the ever tightening grip, and then lost consciousness.

When he opened his eyes he found he was lying upon the floor in the entrance hall of the residence, and he gazed upon two pairs of handcuffs, one of which was clasped around his wrists, while the other held his ankles in their steel embrace, while above him, watching his every movement, was a man dressed in the uniform of a captain of police who in a most menacing manner fingered the trigger of a revolver, which Jim recognized as the same weapon that he had attempted to steal off the parlor table.

Jim could not speak, as his badly crushed throat would not permit this even had he wished to do so, but he further saw the same charitable lady who had been so willing to purchase his last needle case, bending over him, and while she looked at him as he lay there upon the floor before her, handcuffed like a hardened, dangerous criminal, he heard her plead with him. "Boy," she said, while her pitying eyes looked straight into his own, "is there not somewhere in this world a good mother who has taught you that honesty is always the best policy?" And while tears of bitter repentance commenced to course down the poor boy's cheeks she repeated the question, which caused the now heart-broken lad to sob aloud in his anguish.

A moment later the police patrol was heard clanging in the distance—it had been called by telephone. It stopped in front of the house and presently two blue-coats saluted their superior and then picked up the boy, but before they carried him to the waiting police patrol the captain told them that as he had come home for dinner a little earlier than usual, he had divested himself of his heavy pistol and then, while he was taking a mid-day rest upon the parlor lounge he had watched the boy sneaking into the room, picking up the revolver from the center table, and then he pictured to the policemen how he had quietly arisen from the lounge and like a bolt from the blue sky made a prisoner of the chap, whom he described as a most dangerous sneak thief—he did not know the true story of the boy's past nor that not two weeks had elapsed since the same handcuffed lad would have willingly laid down his life before he would have permitted himself to stoop so low as to touch property belonging to another person with the intention of stealing same, nor was the captain acquainted with the fact that a tramp within an even shorter space of time had killed this honesty, had spoiled the future and virtually wrecked the life of the lad by forcing him to become his road kid.

Within an hour's time the plinger gang in their rooms above the slum saloon had been apprised by the subtle and mysterious means which is a sixth sense with criminals, that the missing Jim, who had not shown up for dinner, was behind the bars of the city prison, and afraid that he would "peach" they made haste to vacate their quarters and scattered to the four winds, each jocker taking his road kids with him. Just as they separated, while the other scoundrels tried to console Kansas Shorty for having so quickly been deprived of such a good road kid as Jim had proven himself to be, he cheerily replied to their words of consolation: "There are many more cities like Denver in the States and Canada where we can ply our profession the same as we have here, and there are any number of other people's sons whom I can entrap and can force through fear of exposure and by brutality into becoming tramps, drunkards, beggars and criminals, all at one and the same time."

They carried Jim to the city prison and locked him into a dark dungeon, from which, after several hours of solitary confinement, three detectives took him into the chief of police's office and there pleaded with him to reveal the whereabouts of his jocker, as they were well aware that this lad was merely a tool in the hands of some designing scoundrel, but Jim, as all the other road kids before him have done, refused to divulge the least word that would have caused his jocker's apprehension.

Finding that pleading and threats were unavailing, the officers in their efforts to catch the man "higher up" swore at Jim, then cuffed him and finally, angry at the stubborn silence of the boy, they beat him dreadfully, but even this punishment was in vain for Jim ever repeated in his mind at every cuff and lick he received, that Kansas Shorty had his mother's correct address and that this scoundrel would do far worse than merely murder him, should Jim fail to keep the promise not to tell who was his jocker.

Unable to extort a word from Jim that would lead to the arrest of his jocker, the officers dragged the staggering, heart-broken lad back to his cell and locked him up. When from sheer exhaustion he fell asleep late in the night, he dreamed that Kansas Shorty's grinning face was pressed against his steel-barred cell door. "Jim, Jim," he could distinctly hear the scoundrel say mocking him in his helplessness, "come on, Jim, let us go and peddle needle cases and loot more houses." Jim leaped from his bunk at Kansas Shorty's throat, as if he were a

57

wounded tiger, to strangle with his bare hands the fiend who had so wantonly spoiled his life, but he only gripped the cold steel bars of his cell and awakened, then as he sank back upon the edge of the prison-bunk, he realized that now it was too late—and he burst into bitter tears.

CHAPTER X.
"Slippery, the Yegg."

After Slippery, the Yegg, and Joe had parted company with Kansas Shorty and Jim, they walked leisurely southward upon the railroad track. For some time their conversation lagged, as Slippery was absorbed in thoughts centering upon the boy who was walking by his side. Slippery had up to this moment lived strictly in accord with the laws laid down by the "Code of Crime", the rules of which, although not printed and bound into a costly volume, nor even written, are nevertheless strictly observed by those who defy law and order.

A tradition of this unwritten code was to the effect that a "wise" yegg must never have a minor hoboing with him about the country, as not only would the youngster be of little value when committing a crime and a most decided handicap in making a getaway, but the greatest of danger lay in the fact that should they be arrested, the boy would be more than likely to not only reveal all he knew of the latest exploit of the yegg and tell everything he had seen and heard since their first day's comradeship, but he would undoubtedly turn state's evidence, and help to send the yegg to the penitentiary for a long term. Slippery also weighed the chances which he faced should he by misfortune "ramble" into other "brethren of the gun" who happened to be abroad in the land, especially along oft-traveled routes like those between St. Paul and Chicago, as they would not only frown upon a yegg who had offended the ethics of their clan by having a road kid traveling with him, but they would quickly spread the fact broadcast throughout the land to the detriment of the heretofore good reputation Slippery had enjoyed amongst the numerous members of the "Fraternity of the Dark Lantern."

As a result of these reflections he decided to rid himself of Joe's company as soon as possible, and the easiest and fairest method he could think about to pull himself out of this dilemma was to find a job for the boy upon one of the many farms which were scattered along the right of way.

After having tried for hours to find some sort of a job for the boy, Slippery, thoroughly disgusted at his vain efforts to rid himself of his unwelcome companion, whom he considered by this time a nuisance, decided that the next best plan would be to take Joe to Chicago and find there a employment for him. Then the fact that they were supposed to meet the others at the "big oak" in the evening flashed through his mind, and that perhaps on account of this, Joe would object to hoboing any sort of train.

In furtherance of this plan Slippery visited several additional farm houses to seek employment for the boy, acting after each failure even more discouraged than ever in not being able to find a job, and his disgust increased to such a degree, that it finally became an easy matter for him to have the lad consent that they quit their resultless efforts in this line and instead strive to reach the "big oak" that Slippery assured Joe was growing close to the right of way several miles to the south of them, and there meet the others, whom he had no doubt had had no better success in finding employment.

Slippery now began to paint in most wonderful colors for his younger companion, word-pictures of the grand sights and scenes which were awaiting their arrival at Chicago, and unintentionally drifted into describing the many cases he had heard about, where penniless boys there had risen in a comparatively short time to the rank of multimillionaires.

Joe, who until now paid more attention to the rough, stone ballasted track beneath his feet that made walking a hardship, became greatly interested in the subject that Slippery had reached in his conversation, as it concerned the same matter that Jim and he had threshed out so many times before they left their section home at Rugby, and when Slippery spoke in glowing terms of the many advantages that employment in a large city like Chicago held out to a hustling lad, Joe threw all his troubles to the winds and laid bare to his older comrade every movement since his childhood, and finally came to the point where he and Jim had planned to run away to a city and there by watching for every chance of advancement offered them, and by saving every cent and especially by adhering strictly to honesty, had intended to work their way up the ladder of success until they had reached a respected and independent position. After he had paused to take a second breath, with a true boyish fervor, he commenced to build aircastles as to what he would do when the day arrived when they would not have to look so closely to the saving of their pennies. The more enthusiastically Joe spoke of this bright future, the less he became aware that his hopes had caused the answers he received to his many questions he asked his older companion to become more curt and sullen, nor did he realize that every word he spoke stabbed Slippery's conscience as if it were a two-edged dagger.

Slippery, although he belonged to the the yeggs, had like ninety-nine out of every hundred of his kind, been in his youth a harmless boy who had been enticed by some good-for-nothing tramp to forsake his home, and showing more ambition than to end his days as an alcohol-rotted wreck, had drifted along with criminals, who for the sake of a few dollars or even a handful of unused postage stamps did not hesitate to commit murder, and who had in time taught Slippery the various divisions and subdivisions of their dangerous existence.

Now that Slippery was barely thirty years of age, he was, although young in years, old in crime and had been in many collisions with those who represented law and order, and had served many long terms at hard labor behind the stone walls of state and federal penitentiaries.

One evening, just before Slippery had finished his last sentence, after the prisoners had been locked up for the night, his cell-mate in a spirit of fun suggested that, to while away the time until the lights would be turned low, they compute the average daily wage their crime-steeped lives had earned for them. Although both were regarded by their brethren of crime as most successful in their chosen profession, they found after tedious calculating that the average daily wage of their miserable existence since the day they left their homes had been a fraction less than twenty cents. In this total they did not include the many years they spent behind prison bars, performing, without pay, ambition crushing toil under the eyes of brutal guards, fed upon poor food, sleeping in unhealthy quarters, dressed in coarse, zebra-striped suits and ruled by a most cruel discipline, all of which they were unable to reduce to a dollar and cents basis.

Until that evening his bosom friends had been other equally desperate criminals, as misery loves company, but even few of these could he trust, as "stool pigeons" far outnumbered those whom he could implicitly depend upon and even amongst the few, only too many were snatched from his side by the stern hand of the law to linger for years in penal institutions, if they did not become targets for revolvers or were strangled upon a gallows. The more he thought of this shady side of his past, the more changed became the point of view with which he judged the rest of the world. The laborer whom he saw in the early morning swinging his dinner pail while with light steps he marched to the daily task in mill and factory, and whom he watched in the evening's dusk after the factory sirens had blown the working man's curfew, hurrying home anxious to reach his humble fireside, and for whom heretofore he had only known feelings of deepest contempt, suddenly had become a man who benefitted preciously far more of his life than any yegg he could recall.

A strange yearning to join those who carried the dinner pails and who had homes and firesides of their own made itself felt, and still later this desire to foreswear his past and reform became ever stronger, especially when one day by a singular chance he happened during recess to pass a school house, and stepping behind a tree from where with a wistful look in his eyes he watched the rosy-cheeked, romping children, while at the same time revolting pictures of his own misspent life and thoughts of the far worse to-be-spent future, and the fact that he had been heretofore his own worst enemy came so strongly to his mind that he could barely keep himself from sobbing.

From that evening when he for the first time in his whole life, studied the life of a yegg from a commonsense and strictly commercial side and found it in all its phases a losing game, dated the desire to quit the life of crime when the first opportunity presented itself, but whenever he tried to picture himself as having a happy home of his own, there, like a black cloud suspended in a blue sky, came to him the knowledge that never more could he hide his past, for from the moment that he should endeavor to walk the narrow path, every yegg in the land would point to him as a former brother-in-crime, and gossiping tongues would quickly force him back into the fold, even while with his calloused hands he would be toiling to earn an honest living.

While all of these pictures of his past flashed through his active mind and the desire to be for just one time, a man who needed not to be afraid to associate with honest people, he attentively listened to the boy who was just now unfolding his plans for a bright future, and who was telling about his section home by the side of the railroad track in the midst of the endless prairies of the Dakotas, and although he described the siding of Rugby as being a most desolate place, the desire to reform became almost irresistible to Slippery when Joe told how every evening the railroad laborers returned to their humble quarters worn and tired out by the hard toil of the day, but happy with the satisfaction that by performing their task they had added their share to the world's work for the common good of all humanity.

This was the boy of whose most unwelcome company only a few minutes before Slippery had wished to rid himself as he considered him a serious handicap to his career as a professional criminal, and who was now telling of his plans, how he wished to atone by leading an honest life for the wrong he had done to his widowed mother by leaving his home without her consent, and as he continued to speak of his hopes of a clean and glorious living, the same queer feeling that had attacked him before came with ever increasing force over Slippery, and it almost stunned him when the lad with his true-ringing, youthful voice, exclaimed, "Slippery, you are going to be my partner, for all of us working together can accomplish much more in Chicago to make our way to wealth and fame than we two could. And then, when we have made our fortune, I will want you to come back with us to Rugby and stay with us, even if you have to buy for yourself a prairie farm, for I know mother will wish that you stop with us, because she will always thank you for having taken such good care of her Joe." After he had given vent to this boyish dream he paused, expecting to receive an answer from his older companion, but Slippery only nodded in assent, while at the same time he rubbed his eyes with his hands as if tiny cinders had lodged in them. His emotions caused him to avert his face so Joe could not see the tears of repentance which his hurting conscience forced to run down his cheeks. And then his better self got the master hand over him and he silently swore that at this moment had arrived the oft wished for opportunity for him to forsake the road and quit the crooked game of crime.

Now came Slippery's time to make plans. His first thoughts were to discover the best method to fullfil the promise he had just made to himself to lead a new and different life. The best method as it appeared to him would be for Joe and himself to ramble on to Chicago and there procure employment, as he realized that to separate from his younger companion would mean to him a rapid drifting back into his old ways. This plan looked mighty good and he slyly chuckled as he thought that it would be only a short time until his pay envelope would bulge from the sum to which his wage would quickly increase, for he felt assured that it would be an easy matter for him to be advanced into an ever better salaried position, for a man who had the nerve to attempt to force a living for himself from the world by means of the dangerous ways of crime could easily accomplish anything once his perverted ambitions were directed into the straight and narrow path. But suddenly his smiles ceased and he felt a queer shuddering sensation shake his spine, for he thought of the many criminals who made their headquarters in Chicago, and who would be only too willing to spoil his plans to quit their company and reform, so as to keep others of the brotherhood from quitting the game and thereby making it all the more hazardous for hardened and irreformable criminals to ply their nefarious vocations. He weighed the chances he stood to reform in Chicago and abandoned the scheme as impracticable.

Then Slippery recalled Jim's narrative of his lone prairie section home, and he adroitly questioned the lad and discovered that the country about Rugby was a desolate prairie, that post offices and banks were few, widely scattered and poorly patronized, and that Joe had never heard of any one of these being robbed, nor even a residence or farm house being entered, and when the lad finished by telling of the fertility of the soil and the fact that homesteads could still be had there for the mere filing of the necessary claims, Slippery again became absorbed in his thoughts.

Then he had a vision. He saw himself drilling into a safe. Then came a dull explosion and when the safe's door was torn from its hinges he saw himself upon his knees filling a large bag with the gold coins which poured out of the dynamited treasure box. Then he saw Joe and himself dressed in the best that money could purchase, speeding along aboard a Pullman to Rugby, North Dakota. He felt the hearty hand grip as Joe's mother thanked him for having kept her boy from coming to harm, and when he saw himself the prosperous owner of an immense and well worked farm, he then and there swore a silent but nevertheless solemn oath that after the next successful safe-blowing exploit he would do exactly as this vision had showed him would be the best method to turn over a new page of his life.

"Look out, Slippery, jump for your life!" suddenly came a frightened cry from Joe's lips, and instinctively Slippery followed Joe's example and leaped off the track, upon which they had been so peacefully walking, blissfully ignorant of how close to death they had come. In the next fraction of a second a "Limited" thundered past them, whose ashen-faced engineer was frantically pulling at the whistling cord and blowing the danger signal, while he shook an angry fist at the frightened fellows, who had so narrowly escaped an impending calamity.

"Joe," stammered Slippery, when he again found his voice that from sheer fright failed him for some moments, "boy, you have saved my life and come what may I shall stay and work with you and then after we have made a 'stake' we will go to Rugby and I shall buy a farm and make my home near your home and finish my days in peace and plenty."

'Jump for Your Life!' Suddenly Shouted the Lad, and Both Leaped off the Track, Escaping by a Hair's Breadth Being Struck by the Flying Passenger Train.

From this moment Slippery became a different kind of companion to his younger comrade, and while both now entered into an animated conversation, Joe came to the conclusion that Slippery after all was the best chum he had ever had. They were so busily engaged picturing their futures, that not until evening approached did Joe make any remark concerning the whereabouts of the "big oak" where they were to meet Jim and Kansas Shorty.

They were just approaching a water tank, the destination Slippery intended to reach, and pointing at a large oak close to the track he told Joe that it was the place where he had agreed to meet the others. They went over to it, and after they had made for themselves some coffee, they sat beneath the wide spreading branches of the oak and while dusk turned into night and the calls of the owls echoed over fields and moor, and the moon cast its pale light over the landscape, they patiently waited the arrival of the others. The longer they waited and the more anxious Joe became to meet his twin brother again, the more Slippery denounced Kansas Shorty's tardiness, and when midnight arrived and they heard in the distance to the north of them the rumbling of a train, Slippery had so completely won the confidence of Joe, that the latter consented to accompany the yegg to Chicago without waiting for the arrival of the others, whereupon Slippery tore a page out of his memorandum and after writing on it a brief note, telling Kansas Shorty that he and Joe had rambled into Chicago, and to meet them there, he silenced any rising suspicions Joe might have had that everything was not all right by pinning this note to the trunk of the tree.

When the train, which proved to be a long string of empty, open box cars, pulled southward, after having filled its engine's tender at the water tank, Slippery and Joe had safely stowed themselves away in one of the "empties" and were soon rolling on towards Chicago, and had become a most contented pair of hobo-partners.

Early on the third morning they landed at Chicago, and Joe found that Slippery's tales as to the magnitude of this city had not been exaggerated, for they rode hours and miles upon horseless "cable" cars before Slippery beckoned to Joe to follow him, as they had arrived at their destination, the center of the city's business district.

After eating their breakfast in a restaurant, they sauntered through the streets to see the sights. While they walked aimlessly about the city, Slippery acted at times so strangely that he called the attention of Joe to him, who did not suspect the reason of his singular demeanor, nor that he was walking with a man who in police circles had earned a well merited reputation of being one of the most desperate criminals in the land. Whenever Slippery would spot a policeman ahead of him he would turn into an alley or by-way to avoid passing the guardian of the law. At other times, just after they had passed some well dressed and often really benign looking citizen, Slippery would roughly nudge him and whisper, "that was one of those 'fly mugs'—a detective", and then it would be some moments before he reverted to his former cheerfulness, proving to Joe how much he feared or despised those who uphold the law.

The ringing of the church bells had just announced the noon hour, when Slippery was stopped in the street by a neatly attired gentleman, who, after they had most cordially shaken hands, entered into a whispered conversation, which Joe overheard.

"Hello, Slippery, old boy, when did you find your way back to Chicago?" were the first words of the stranger's greeting, who acted as if he were greatly pleased with the return of Joe's pal to the "Windy City." "I too am glad to be once more where one's eyes do not tire looking into nothingness, bounded only by the horizon and the blue sky," answered Slippery, and then in a whisper, he added: "Say, Boston Frank, give me a square tip where Bunko Bill's gang is, so I can find a temporary hangout until I get straight as to the lay of the land." "Oh, is that what you wish to know, Slippery? Well they are in a private flat on South Clark, just below LaSalle Street, second house from the corner, on the fifth floor, and a dandy place at that, but," here he paused and with an ill-disguised look of resentment he stared at Joe and then queried: "Slippery, whose boy have you toting along with you?" And as Slippery did not promptly answer him he added with contempt in his voice, "I always understood that only a low-lived plinger dragged a road kid about with him and never a proper crook." Then to Joe's terror, he heard the man whom he had until this moment taken to be as honorable as his own late father answer: "Boston Frank, this lad is the wisest and shrewdest young crook that ever walked the streets of Chicago." This explanation pleased Boston Frank, who now asked Slippery to introduce him to the lad, which the former did, using his new nickname, "Dakota Joe." Listening to their further conversation, to his horror Joe became for the first time aware that Slippery was not a man looking for an honest job, but a criminal whose dislike for the police, which he had so openly manifested, was the natural result of the life he had been leading. Joe decided to keep this unpleasant discovery to himself, as he was a penniless lad in the center of an immense city.

When they parted company with Boston Frank, Slippery and Joe found the house that he had described to be the "gang's" hangout, and after they had climbed five flights up a narrow stairway, Slippery rang the door bell of a flat. A shutter in the panel of the door that fitted so perfectly into an opening that Joe did not observe its presence before, was withdrawn and from behind a heavy wire screen a pair of glistening, suspicious eyes searched their faces, and then a voice demanded what they desired. Instead of an answer Slippery gave some differently sounding knocks upon the panel above the screened opening and whispered, "It's I, Slippery, the yegg."

Joe could distinctly hear the same person who had carefully replaced the shutter over the once more invisible spy-opening unbolt, then unlock and finally slowly open the door, and after she, a middle-aged woman, had again most suspiciously scanned the features of her visitors, she permitted Slippery and Joe to slip within the slightly opened door, that she promptly shut, and then bolted and carefully locked, as if the flat, instead of a home for human beings was a safe-deposit vault of an immensely rich bank.

"Hello, Marie," Slippery addressed the woman after she had tried the door knob to assure herself that the steel sheeted door was as correctly closed as before she opened it, "how are you and the rest of the gang?" And while they shook hands Joe looked about in the semi-darkness of the hallway trying to see some members of the gang Slippery had spoken about when he inquired of Boston Frank as to their whereabouts, and about whom he had just repeated the question, which to Joe seemed odd because there was not a sound to be heard in the flat, that, as it was supposed to be the home of a "gang", should have at least shown these signs of human habitation.

After the woman and Slippery had exchanged other brief greetings all three went towards the rear of the hallway, and here she opened a door and bade them enter, and by the brilliant illumination they saw it was the dining room of the fiat. Around its well provisioned dinner table were seated a number of men and women who in a most friendly, but noise avoiding manner, greeted Slippery and while they questioned him as to his latest movements, they gave Joe a chance to recover from the surprise that completely shocked him, when he discovered that this strangely secluded flat was the home of seven men and four women, all of the latter—with the exception of the woman who had opened the door—being barely more than young girls.

CHAPTER XI.
"The Wages of Sin is Death."

"Look here, friends," remarked one of the men seated at the table, who was dressed in the height of fashion, and later proved to be the leader of the others, after he had greeted Slippery and had for a brief moment gazed at Joe, "Slippery has brought a road kid along with him, no doubt intending to imitate the ways of the accursed plingers and add another tramp to those who already hobo about the country." Slippery, to whom this tart rebuke was addressed, now explained that the lad by his side was his "pal", and not his road kid; this explanation seemed to satisfy the speaker for he stretched out his hand and greeted Joe in a most cordial manner, while Slippery introduced him to the party, not by his honest Christian name, but by his road name, "Dakota Joe". But the next moment a far greater surprise was in store for the boy when Slippery commenced to introduce him to the well attired gentlemen and richly gowned ladies, whom he supposed, judging by their general appearance, were far removed from the level they had chosen for themselves, for presently Slippery announced the name of the "gentleman" with whom he had just shaken hands as "Bunko Bill", and Joe's unpleasant suspicions that he had been led into a nest of human vipers were greatly increased when his pal called off the names of the other inmates of the flat. The nearest fellow was "Brooklyn Danny, the Dip"; the next one went by the name of "Buffalo Johnny, the Strong Arm Man"; the fourth responded to "Ohio Jack, the Sneak"; a neat looking fellow who sported a diamond stud upon his shirt bosom answered to the appropriate name of "Diamond Al"; while the criminal tendencies of the sixth were plainly stamped in his nickname, "Niagara Swifty, the Shop Lifter", while the last one, a red-haired, wary-looking chap answered to the rather suggestive name of "Atlanta Jerry, the Hold-Up."

Joe, who had heard at home the section men tell about the "monicker" every tramp bore, could not help but note that these "names-de-crime" which Slippery had just now given as the ones with which these gentlemen addressed each other, so very closely resembled those used by the hoboes that perhaps every one of the men before him had formerly been a road kid.

The boy's astonishment was greatly increased when next Slippery introduced the "ladies". The one who so cautiously opened the door for their entrance was honored by the name of "Dippy Marie"; the second on account of the color of her hair was known as "Red Annie"; while a third was titled "Noisy Jane", and the last, the youngest and best looking one of them, went by the nickname of "Babe".

After this introduction Bunko Bill invited Slippery and Joe to make their home with them during their sojourn in Chicago, which offer was readily accepted and then all sat down to dine. After dinner Slippery under the pretense of wishing to show Joe the city, managed to keep out of complications which might have been caused by some of the inmates too closely questioning the lad, and he took the boy for a walk to the nearby shores of Lake Michigan.

After Joe had enjoyed for some time the beauty of the marine scenery that spread like a gigantic panorama before his eyes, he broke the silence by bluntly asking Slippery how and when they were to meet his brother Jim. Slippery assured Joe and quieted him by saying that it would be merely a matter of days before they would meet Jim in the street in the same manner that they had met Boston Frank.

They returned to the flat in time to join the others at supper, and after this had been served Joe wondered why one after another, all the members of the gang cautiously slipped out of the door and vanished down the stairway with the sole exception of "Dippy Marie", who showed them to their bedroom.

In the morning Boston Frank made a call at the flat, and behind locked doors had a long conference with Slippery and the others. After his visit Slippery became a busy man and Joe watched him oiling, filing and tempering a collection of jimmies, nippers, wedges, pliers, saws, and other such tools for which an expert mechanic could find a proper use. When Joe carelessly picked up a small bottle that stood upon the table before Slippery, the yegg's face turned pale, and then he explained to the boy who too commenced to shudder the longer he listened, that the harmless looking liquid in the bottle was fearfully dangerous nitro-glycerine.

The following afternoon Boston Frank made a second visit and then he and Slippery, each carrying a heavy satchel filled with the tools Slippery had so carefully looked after, followed by Joe, around whose left leg they had bandaged, despite his most vehement protests, the small bottle containing the deadly explosive, left the flat. They took a street car to the railroad station, where Boston Frank purchased tickets to Dixon, one of the prettiest and most hustling cities in western Illinois. Soon they were rolling out of the railroad yards and across the fertile plains and arrived at their destination late in the night.

They left the train from the rear platform of the last Pullman, and climbed to the ground from the opposite side of the station platform, and after they had hurriedly walked about a mile in the darkness, Boston Frank stopped at a barn, and while Slippery and Joe walked ahead, he noiselessly opened the barn door and after hitching the owner's fastest horse to his best buggy he leisurely overtook the others and made them climb in, after they had placed the heavy satchels in the buggy's body, and then he carefully drove the horse on into the night.

During their conversation, which Joe overheard, Boston Frank mentioned to Slippery that the "P.-O." had been reported to be a regular mint, and he repeatedly assured him that no one was sleeping in the "P.-O." as he had tried several nights in succession to purchase tobacco at the "P.-O.", but his knocks were not answered.

At a cross-roads country store they stopped and here Joe understood what Boston Frank had meant with "P.-O.", as it bore a large sign that had the words "Post Office" painted upon it.

While Boston Frank hitched the horse and buggy to a nearby tree, Slippery carried the heavy satchels containing the tools to the rear of the store, while he ordered Joe to carefully unwrap the nitro-glycerine bottle from his leg, which the boy gladly did to be rid of the dangerous explosive, and then handed it to Slippery.

Joe, who had not yet the least inkling what sort of mysterious night work was contemplated by his older companions, suddenly came to the realization of his own danger when Slippery in a decidedly unfriendly manner, roughly commanded him to stand guard in front of the store, and after he had placed the lad so he could scan the different roads, he did something that has made more blood thirsty desperadoes out of harmless boys than any other trick, he pressed a cocked, large calibered revolver into the unsuspecting boy's hand and curtly ordered him, under pain of losing his own life if he failed to obey this order, to blaze away at any approaching human being. Then he disappeared towards the rear of the building.

For a moment Joe's brain worked overtime, especially when he looked at the murder tool the other fellow had placed into his trembling hand and he promptly decided to cast the pistol into the middle of the roadway and run for his life to escape not only the clutches of these fellows, whom he now realized were desperate robbers, but to escape a possibly far worse fate. Just as he started to follow out this idea, Slippery stepped around the corner, and after he once more warned the lad not to falter in shooting to kill, he gave Joe a spool of fine copper wire to hold and when the surprised boy wished to know the reason, he showed Joe where he had the other end of the same wire twisted about his wrist, and cautioned him to hold it taut and that every time he gave the wire a sharp pull the boy should answer with the same signal, and that if he saw any-one approaching several sharp pulls should be the danger signal. Then he again left the lad, and whenever he tugged on the wire Joe answered with the agreed signal, and by this simple means Slippery had not only forced a harmless boy to do dangerous outpost duty, and was assured that he was always on guard, but what was most important, he had a noiseless danger signal that, even should the boy fail to kill somebody, he would thus notify the robbers that all was not well and give them plenty of time and a far better chance to make their getaway than the boy himself had, especially if he "shot to kill", as he had been commanded to do, which would have meant a long term behind the prison bars if not a trip by the route of the hangman's rope.

While Joe had thus been forced to become their involuntary accomplice, the two yeggs pried open the rear entrance of the store, and then Slippery worked at his profession of safe blowing. When all had been made ready to explode the charge, they carried the satchels with their tools out of the store and placed them in the buggy and made everything ready for an instant escape. Boston Frank unhitched the horse and held it by the head, while Slippery went back to the store, lit the fuse and then stood at the rear door until an explosion, which seemed to tear the store asunder told the waiting yeggs that the moment to commence their dangerous harvest had arrived. While Boston Frank had trouble to quiet the madly plunging, frightened horse, Slippery dove into the store to emerge again an instant later choking, sneezing and almost blinded just as if he had dynamited a box loaded with powdered red pepper instead of a common fireproof safe. Foiled in stealing the contents of the safe, amid awful curses, he climbed into the buggy and called to Joe to jump upon its rear, and while they heard all around them loud calls and even pistol shots of the farmers, who had been aroused out of their slumbers, Boston Frank turned into the highway leading back to Dixon and the race for their liberty commenced.

They dashed down the wagon road at top speed, Boston Frank ever urging the horse on to greater efforts, as in speed lay their only salvation.

Passing the first farm house which fronted upon the wagon road, they could see by the light cast by a lantern that stood beside him upon the porch, a man dressed in his night robe raise a revolver and after taking a careful aim at the approaching buggy, just as they were in line with him, discharge point blank in quick succession its six messengers of death into their midst. But Boston Frank did not slacken the pace, on the contrary he urged the horse to ever greater speed.

Not a word was exchanged by the inmates of the buggy during this race, and for several miles farther they drove at the utmost speed, then the horse's terrific gait commenced to slacken, and now that they were beyond the aroused neighborhood, Boston Frank slowed the horse and turned in at a road crossing to throw possible pursuers upon a wrong trail.

Just as they realized how close an escape they had, Slippery keeled over against Boston Frank and said hoarsely: "Frank, for mercy's sake take me where I can get a drink of water. The fellow who fired at us from the first farm house hit his mark, for I am shot." "Slippery, old boy," now queried Boston Frank, not believing that such a dire calamity had overtaken them, "you are joking, aren't you?" And then, when Slippery did not answer, he looked into his pal's face and saw there the pallor of death while two dark lines emerging from the corner of his mouth caused by the wounded man's life blood, trickling away, proved to him that his comrade in crime had only too accurately spoken the bitter truth. Now he coughed and when Boston Frank saw a stream of blood shoot out of the wounded man's mouth and heard a choking noise in his throat, he readily recognized the nature of the hurt and that Slippery had been shot through his lungs.

Boston Frank in sheer desperation again urged the rapidly tiring horse to one last effort, but soon the best speed he could get out of the animal was a slow trot. Again Slippery most piteously begged for a drink of water, and taking a desperate chance, when he saw in the darkness an open gate that led into a field, he guided the tired horse into it, and after Joe had closed the gate behind them he drove ahead until a thick thorn hedge stopped further progress. Here they lifted the wounded man out of the buggy and laid him upon the ground. He continued to plead most piteously for a cooling drink of water to appease his torturing fever thirst. "Joe," cautioned Boston Frank, after he had securely tied the horse to the hedge, "you take care of poor Slippery until I return with my derby filled with water, as I cannot bear to listen longer to the poor fellow's heart-rending appeals." Then he disappeared into the night, resolved to find water at any price.

"Joe, Joe, come here, Joe," the lad heard Slippery weakly calling a moment later, and he knelt beside the wounded man and asked him what he desired. Just then Slippery could not answer, as he was again vomiting blood, and Joe tried to ease his breathing by elevating his head with boughs he broke from the hedge.

"Joe," the wounded fellow called again, "where are you, Joe?" The boy placed his hand in the outstretched, searching hands of Slippery, who feebly pressed them with his own and said, "Joe, I know I am mortally wounded, and want you to make me, a dying man, a promise. I meant to forsake crime and live the life of an honest man for your sake after we had successfully pulled off this job—my last one." He paused a moment and then continued, "I took you with us, so when you and I went to your home in Rugby you would never forget that you had been my accomplice and would not be apt to peach on me. I know that the wound I received is the just punishment for the greatest wrong mortal man can commit, that of leading a harmless boy astray." Again he paused, as if his troubled conscience overpowered him, and then with a renewed effort that heavily taxed his fast ebbing vitality, he added, "Joe, for the love you bear for your mother, of whom you have spoken so often, swear now, before the Almighty, that you will from this moment forward shun the three evils which have brought me to this, and which are 'Bums, Booze and Boxcars', and that you will not further associate with the criminals at the flat, for if you return to them, on account of this night's work you will be forever one of their number." And there in the solitude of the night, kneeling beside his dying companion, with his arms uplifted towards the starry firmament, Joe solemnly swore that he would beware of "Bums, Booze and Boxcars", and quit the very people whose acquaintance he had made through Slippery.

And there in the Solitude of the Night, Kneeling Beside His Dying Companion, Joe Solemnly Swore to forever forsake the 'Road.'

For a moment all was silence, which was interrupted only by the gurgling of the blood as it welled up into the mortally wounded yegg's throat, then came the pitifully human appeal from the lips of the dying man, "Joe, where are you, Joe? Do not leave me alone, Joe, now that all have left me and everything is so dark before my eyes." Then after a brief pause he painfully stammered, "Joe, find your brother Jim, then both of you go back to your mother and be once more her boys." He again became silent and then, now that it was too late, he plainly showed, that although he was a despised yegg, there was one place in this wide world where there would be one true friend waiting in vain for his return, for he slowly added, "Joe, believe me, there is no friend like mother and no place like home."

Then came another hemorrhage and a stream of his life blood shot into the air and then, with a last effort, he drew Joe's hands to his parched, suffering lips, and while he covered them with kisses, the rattling in his throat increased, then decreased, and finally stopped—he had expired.

When Boston Frank returned with the water, he only found his dead pal, as Joe, horror stricken by the dead man's glassy stare, by the blood covered corpse, by the quietude of the night and all the horrors which had transpired, had fled into the night as if furies and demons were pursuing him, bent only upon placing as much space as possible between his living self and the gruesome tragedy he had left behind. He climbed over fences and forced his way through hedges; forded creeks and swam streams, until from his frantic exertions he became so completely exhausted that when he fell into a clump of bushes he was unable to rise, and gradually sank into a deep sleep.

Then a strange dream came to him. He dreamed he was a prisoner locked up in a narrow cell, and that he saw Slippery, the yegg's face pressed against its cross-barred steel door, while on both sides of him stood officers of the law. They were leading him to the gallows, upon which he had been condemned to expiate his crime, and now on his way to face his doom he had stopped to bid Joe a last farewell, and Joe could distinctly hear his words: "Good-bye, Joe, do not do as I did, who when a youngster ran away from a good home to follow Bums, Booze and Boxcars, but go back to your waiting mother before it is too late, for remember, 'The Wages of Sin is Shameful Death'."

CHAPTER XII.
"Scattered to the Winds."

The sun stood high in the heavens when Joe awakened, and it was some moments before he remembered the horrible occurrences of the preceding night. But most vividly of all he remembered the solemn promise he had made to his dying pal and to strengthen himself in his resolve to strictly live up to his pledge, he fell upon his knees and repeated the solemn oath.

At a rippling brook he washed and removed every trace of the ordeal he had passed through, and then inquired from a farmer the direction to the railroad station at Dixon, where he intended to hop a train to Chicago and, arriving in the city, find a job so he could support himself honestly, while keeping on a lookout for his missing brother Jim.

After an hour's walk he arrived at the railroad station and found a crowd surging about a baggage truck which stood upon the station platform, and when he managed to push his way through the throng he found that the people were staring at a blood soaked blanket that covered a carcass of some sort. Joe only stopped for a moment, for when one of the men, more curious than the others, lifted up a corner of the blanket, Joe gazed into the lifeless features of Slippery, the yegg, and forced by his emotions he retreated quickly to another part of the platform.

Here he overheard some of the citizens discussing the post office robbery, and he heard them say that the railroad and city policemen had identified the dead robber as one of the most dangerous criminals in the land for whose apprehension "dead or alive", the government offered a large reward. He also heard that the same country store post office had been dynamited twice in the past three months, and that the postmaster had set a trap with the aid of his neighbors, to give the next gang of burgling yeggs a hot reception.

Presently a loud shout was heard and the crowd made a rush to the front of the station. Joe followed and saw a dirt covered man, securely manacled to an officer, entering the waiting room. Joe instantly recognized Boston Frank, and heard that he had been caught by a farmer's posse, who, following a trail of blood that had dripped from the buggy, had surprised Boston Frank while he was busy at work burying the satchels containing the burglar tools.

Joe caught Boston Frank's eye and forthwith pushed himself alongside the yegg. While the officer to whom he was manacled paid close attention to the postmaster, who told him that although yeggs had spoiled his safe for a third time, he had protected his own and the government's valuables by having placed a quart bottle of formaldehyde in the safe, Boston Frank contrived to whisper to Joe that he had Slippery's purse in his hip pocket, and for him to take it and keep its contents, as he himself would have little use for cash in the penitentiary, for a long term now stared him in the face, and he ordered Joe to purchase a ticket and take the first train leaving for Chicago and to warn the others, as the officers, while searching him had found an incriminating letter that bore upon its envelope the correct address of the gang's hangout.

Joe did as Boston Frank had directed, and a moment later he had, unobserved, abstracted a well-filled purse from the latter's pocket and hid it in his own. He then made his way to the ticket window and called for a ticket to Chicago. When he pulled out the purse that Boston Frank had told him belonged to the slain criminal, he almost dropped it from sheer surprise, as he instantly recognized it as his own purse, the very one that had been stolen from him at the Golden Rule Hotel, and the loss of which had started all of his misfortunes. He paid for the ticket and then in a secluded spot he counted the contents of the purse, which proved to be a windfall to the penniless lad, as it amounted to twelve dollars.

While he waited for the arrival of the train, marvel as he might, he could not solve the riddle connected with the strange return of his purse that had so mysteriously managed to come back to its rightful owner after having disappeared at a place five hundred miles removed from Dixon, Illinois.

He rode to Chicago on the same train upon which the government officers were bringing the corpse of the slain robber, and while Boston Frank was chained to a seat in the smoking car, Joe sat silently in the first-class coach, thinking of the lucky escape he had had and ever and anon repeating the oath he had made to the now lifeless clay in the baggage car ahead.

While Joe was thus occupied he must have attracted the attention of one of the train men, who good-naturedly stopped to chat with him, and inquired where he was going. Joe told him that Chicago was his destination, and innocently added that he intended to find employment in the city. "Say, kid," the good-natured brakeman advised him, more as a huge joke than in a serious vein, "if you cannot find anything better, hit my boss for a job." And then he gave Joe the correct address of his superior.

When the train arrived at the Chicago terminal, Joe boarded a street car that brought him quickly to the flat where he intended to acquaint its inmates with the misfortune that had overtaken Slippery and Boston Frank, and also to deliver the verbal message the latter had given him. To his surprise he found the front of the house in which the flat was located kept clear of public traffic by a cordon of policemen, while several police patrols were backed against the curb, and were not only loaded with the handcuffed criminals, who had been caught like rats in a trap, upon the telegraphic advice of the Dixon police authorities, but with thousands of dollars worth of stolen property that had been found in trunks and other hiding places.

Her Emotions Got the Better of Her and She Placed Her Arms Around the Sobbing Lad's Neck and Kissed Him.

While Joe stood in the crowd watching the finish of those who had transgressed the law, with far better reasons than the curious idlers about him could suspect, he felt someone sharply pull his coat sleeve. He felt himself turning ashen-gray from fright as he thought some detective had recognized him, and when the same sharp pull was repeated, trembling with fear, he turned to see who it was that knew him in Chicago, and recognized that his dread was groundless as it was "Babe" who had pulled his sleeve, the youngest girl in the den of the thieves, who luckily happened to be away from home when the police commenced the raid of the flat.

"Come, Joe," she whispered, "I want to speak to you." He followed the girl and both walked to the nearby shore of Lake Michigan, where he repeated to her word for word everything that had occurred since he last saw her at the flat, and when he remarked that both of them should thank a kind Providence that had kept them out of the hands of the police, tears trickled down their cheeks, while they gazed out over the restless waters of the lake.

It was "Babe" who broke the silence by remarking: "We are indeed lucky, Joe. Just think of what would have been our fate had we been arrested with the others. You would have been sent to a penal institution to emerge years later an ex-convict, a marked man forever afterwards, while I would have been sent to a home where I would have been forced to associate with the most degraded wretches. I was only seventeen last month and was sent from a faraway western city to a boarding school in the east, where the "blue stocking" matrons made the unfettered life that I had learned to love at home such a misery for me, that I ran away and came to Chicago to seek employment. I fell in with evil company, but, thank God, I have yet enough common sense left to know when to quit, and that is right now. For obvious reasons, I am not going to tell you my address, but," here she turned and out of a hiding place in her dress pulled a fair-sized roll of greenbacks, and then she continued, "I have managed to look out for a day just like this one and have saved a few dollars so I could get back home in the west, and" now she peeled a hundred dollar bill from the roll she held in her hand, "I want you to accept this sum and forget that you ever met me." Here her emotions got the best of her and she put her arms around Joe's neck, who was sobbing, being unable to express in any other manner his appreciation of the girl's generosity, and after she had kissed the boy she whispered: "Joe, for the sake of your mother I want you to swear that you will never again become a companion of criminals." Joe repeated to her the same solemn oath he had pledged to the dying Slippery, and promised that he would faithfully adhere to it as long as he lived. When he finished, for the want of something better to give her as a souvenir, he emptied the purse that had so strangely come back to him and made the girl accept it as a token of his gratitude for her timely help, when a mere dozen dollars stood between him and temptation.

After making Joe promise that he would not attempt to follow her, she bade him farewell and walked to the nearest street crossing, and while Joe was busy wiping his eyes with one of his hands, he waved her farewell with the other until she mounted a street car and was whirled beyond his vision.

After Joe had furnished himself with a proper outfit of clothing, and all the other things required by a young man who intends to find a respectable position, he engaged a room at a first-class hotel. He ate his supper in company with honest people and later retired for the night. He turned off the light, and while he lay there between the sheets waiting for sleep to overtake him, the fearful experiences of the last two days followed one another through his agitated mind just as if they were moving pictures. When he came to the scene where he knelt by the side of the flying yegg and solemnly swore to forever quit the path Slippery had shown him, he felt a strange power drag him out of the bed, force him to kneel upon the floor and repeat the sacred promise to shun Bums, Booze and Boxcars and then, when he went again to bed, it was only a few moments until he was soundly sleeping.

CHAPTER XIII.
"Where is my Brother James"

On the following morning after he had breakfasted, he carefully copied all suitable advertisements inserted in the daily papers and set out to find employment, resolved to accept the very first job offered him, having profited by his Minneapolis experience when he and Jim refused many offers of employment which for the moment did not look good to them, but for which on the following day they actually begged.

Filled with hope to quickly land a good job, he called at the different addresses, and, although he walked for hours up and down the streets and avenues, everywhere he inquired the place had been secured by some other person who had called earlier in the day. When afternoon approached, wearied by the resultless job-hunt and discouraged by his continued misfortune, he sank upon a bench in a city park to take a rest.

While listlessly watching the passersby a touch of homesickness almost got the mastery of him. He was just at the point of deciding if it would not be best for him while yet he had the funds to do so, to purchase a ticket back to Rugby and ask his mother's forgiveness. He even arose from the bench to put this idea into execution, but he only made a few steps when he faltered and returned to his seat, the courage to face his mother without his brother James failed him. To find James now became his one desire, but think of whatever scheme he might, it seemed that to have patience and wait to meet him in Chicago was the only method he could discover.

Just then, whistling a lively tune and with a toothpick saucily sticking out of one corner of his mouth, a small Western Union Messenger boy, dressed in all the brass buttoned glory of his snappy uniform, passed the tormented Joe, and somehow the latter's dejected countenance did not please the telegram carrier, and he greeted him with a withering, sneering look that caused Joe to double his fist within his pockets, aching to have it out with the fresh fellow. But before he could muster sufficient anger to start trouble, the messenger boy, no doubt fearing a sound thrashing, quickened his steps and hastened beyond the danger zone. Joe watched him until he passed around a street corner and wondered what caused him to be so overbearing, and just then the uniform of the messenger reminded him of the advice the brakeman gave him on the train, that should he be unable to find a job to tackle his superintendent for employment. He consulted his notebook into which he had entered the address, and taking a street car, a few minutes later he climbed the stairway of a large railroad office building and quickly found himself in the ante-room of the railroad ruler's office.

When his turn came he entered the superintendent's office, whom he found to be a very kindly spoken gentleman, and brought matters to a quick head by blandly asking him for employment. The superintendent smiled to see a youngster like Joe daring to ask him, the master of thousands of employees, for a job, but Joe quickly convinced him that he was able to do a man's work and told how his late father had been a railroad employee at the time of his demise. The superintendent became interested in the open-faced lad, who most insistently pleaded to be given a chance to prove his desire to make good.

In those days, the railroad companies were not so strict in the hiring of their employees as they are at present, and when the superintendent asked Joe what sort of job he thought he could fill, the latter, remembering the natty uniform of the passenger train's crew, promptly replied that a brakeman's job aboard a passenger train would just suit him, which answer caused the superintendent to break out into a hearty laugh, after he had told Joe that he was several sizes too small to fill that position. But Joe was entirely too much in earnest to be turned away this easily, and drawing himself to his full height, he pleaded that, as he had no home and neither touched tobacco nor strong drink, he should at least be given a trial, and then finished his appeal by telling the superintendent that a young, live and accommodating trainman was preferred by the patrons of every railroad to a cranky one.

This last statement pleased the superintendent so well that he told Joe to report a week after date in a regulation uniform and that he should have a chance to prove his side of the argument. Joe thanked the superintendent for his kindness and after he closed the office door he jumped down the stairway three steps at a time, so happy was he. In fact he realized that he had not only found a job that would decently support him, but one that strictly conformed with his somewhat restless disposition, as it permitted him to travel to his heart's content aboard the flying trains, giving him at the same time a chance to earn an honest living and see a bit of the world.

He gave a tailor a "hurry" order for a trainman's uniform, and when he reported on the appointed day at the superintendent's office, he was put in charge of a conductor who quickly became his fatherly friend, because Joe did everything required of him in a most satisfactory manner. Each pay day he placed a large percentage of his salary in a savings bank, and as his wages were from time to time increased, he soon became the owner of a comfortable bank account.

He always kept a sharp lookout for his brother Jim, but five years rolled around in which time he found no trace of his missing brother. Finally he was attacked by a severe case of homesickness; somehow he felt a strange loneliness come over him, and the picture of his mother could not be effaced from his mind, and fearing as much as ever to return home without his twin brother, he finally wrote a long letter, pleading for her forgiveness and inquiring if anything had been heard from James since they left home together. He wrote his own address in the upper corner of the envelope and dropped the letter into a mail box. But from the moment the letter left his hands, his anxiety while waiting for an answer became such a burden that he was unable to attend to his duties, and had to ask for a lay-off. As hours were added to hours and days to days without an answer arriving, the strain of the suspense finally became so fearful that mute desperation was written in every line of his face, and to end the misery he was busily packing his suitcase ready to leave for Rugby, letter or no letter, the following morning and there upon his knees plead with his mother to forgive his boyish prank, when someone knocked on the door and when he opened it he found it was his landlady who handed him a letter, and he recognized it as being the same one he had addressed to his mother at Rugby, but there was this time written across its face: "Moved to Canada. Present address unknown."

Joe stared at the letter for some moments as if dazed, then he locked the door, and when on the following afternoon his landlady knocked to inquire if anything was wanted he opened it. His bed was still unruffled, showing that he had not occupied it during the night, and when she saw the same letter she had brought to him, its writing blurred and tear-stained, lying open upon the dresser, and noted the red and swollen eyes and woe-begone expression of Joe's face, her motherly heart quickly surmised the pitiful drama that had been enacted behind the closed door of the room. She stepped close to the broken-hearted man, who was sitting upon a chair, mutely holding his head between his hands, and while she lightly stroked his hair she pleaded with him to go to the street, as she thought that mingling with the crowds would prove the best heart-balm for him.

Joe took his kind landlady's advice, and while walking about the streets he felt that the pangs of remorse for the prank which had deprived him of his good mother were less severe, and when he began to feel more like his former self he retraced his steps to his lodging house.

When he reached South Clark Street, his progress was blocked by a jam of vehicle traffic. The ever increasing crowd of delayed people forced Joe into the vestibule of one of the many slum saloons abounding in that locality, and here he watched the mounted police hard at work trying to again open the thoroughfare. While he thus passed the time until he could cross the street, he was accosted by a typical Chicago rum-soaked bum. "Say, friend," the semi-maudlin wretch pleaded while he edged most uncomfortably close to Joe, "would you mind assisting a hungry fellow who has not eaten a square meal in a week?" More for the sake of getting rid of his unpleasant company, than from a desire to accord charity, Joe went into his trouser pockets for a small coin to hand to the beggar, but while fumbling for the money he caused his trainman's cap to fall to the pavement. He reached down and picked it up, and when he straightened himself he pulled out a dime and handed it to the beggar, who, instead of accepting the proffered donation, disdainfully pushed aside the hand holding the alms and stepping closer he almost insultingly leered into Joe's face. "Say, McDonald," he hissed, "when did you make your getaway?" Before the astonished Joe could utter a single word the tramp pointed at Joe's trainman's cap and added: "I see you are working now for the Chicago & North-Western Railroad," and when still no sign of recognition came from Joe's mouth he in a most threatening manner finished: "Do they know your record over there?"

'Say, Friend,' Pleaded the Semi-Maudlin Beggar, 'Would You Mind Assisting a Hungry Fellow Who Has Not Eaten a Square Meal in a Week?'

Joe, although he trembled with ill-suppressed rage at this street beggar's impudence to openly insult him in such barefaced manner, held his peace for the moment, as he tried in vain to fathom how and where the mendicant had learned to call him by his correct name. To wring this information from the sodden wretch was his first purpose. "Say, fellow," Joe almost pleasantly asked the beggar, "who told you that my name is McDonald?" "Did you think I did not recognize you?" replied the bum in a most insolent tone while at the same time he pointed his hand at Joe's birthmark. "When you bent forward to pick up your cap I remembered you the moment I put my eyes on that streak of white hair," and then, sure that he had before him a victim whom he could blackmail with perfect impunity, he inquired, "Have you been back to Rugby since I saw you the last time, and say, McDonald, how are the chances for your helping a poor friend to the price of a meal and a bunking place for the night?"

Joe felt greatly relieved when he heard the fellow's more familiar talk, as it seemed to prove that the beggar had been one of his late father's section laborers, and he searched his pockets once more and pulled out a silver dollar and pressed the coin into the man's outstretched palm, and then, wondering why he did not even deign to thank him for this generous gift he inquired if he had lately been back to Rugby, and if he ever heard what had become of his mother, Mrs. McDonald. Instead of an answer to his question the beggar straightened himself to his full height, "So you have not been home?" the bum mocked in a most impudent manner, "a little scared to show up amongst the folks at home with that soiled record chalked behind their honest family name, eh?" As yet no reply came from the trainman's trembling lips, still under the impression that he was speaking to Joe's twin brother, the bum added, while a most diabolical grin spread over his ugly visage, "Haven't peddled needle cases lately, have you?" "I do not understand what you are referring to," the now thoroughly mystified Joe interrupted the beggar, "I have never peddled a needle case in all my life." "Trying to wiggle yourself out of your past, eh?" the vagrant scornfully retorted, and thinking that his victim was trying to slip out of his net, he continued, "guess you think you can fool this old plinger and try to work the 'innocent' game on your old jocker, eh?"

Joe again insisted that he did not understand what the fellow was trying to say, and tiring of the unpleasant conversation he blandly asked the beggar if he were not somewhat rum crazed. "Call me rum crazed," the wretch shrieked in towering rage, feeling that his victim was getting the better of the argument, that he intended should form a base upon which he would later collect blackmail, and while he shook his dirty fist in Joe's face, he added, "I, crazy? How dare you call me crazy? I, Kansas Shorty, the plinger?" Then he stepped back a pace and while his hideous, rum-bloated face was made all the more repulsive by his malevolent eyes with which he glared at the shuddering Joe, who only now, that the fiend had revealed his name-de-road recalled and recognized in the person of the beggar, the tramp who had taken charge of his brother James.

While the rogue was yet gloating over the apparent discomfort his words had caused, Joe suddenly threw himself upon the vagabond, and while he bore him to the pavement and while his hands throttled the viper's throat, he shrieked into the beggar's ears. "I am Joseph McDonald, and you die on this spot unless you tell me what you have done with my brother James." They struggled desperately, one to free himself from the strangle hold, while Joe wished to force a confession from the fellow beneath him whose staring eyes were bulging out of his skull, and whose face had commenced to turn a bluish-black.

Quickly the usual city crowd gathered about the fighting men and a second later the slum saloon in front of which they were battling, emptied its filthy scum into the street, all anxious to enjoy the combat. Some of the plingers amongst this riff-raff must have recognized their mate, and thinking that the trouble was merely a case of a street beggar insulting a citizen, and noting that this one wore the hated uniform of a railroad man—every tough's sworn enemy —they made common cause and the next moment Joe saw a heavy beer bottle descending upon his head, then all was darkness.

When he regained consciousness he was lying upon the floor of the slum saloon, with his pockets turned inside out and his watch missing, and a dull pain almost bursting his skull. He staggered to his feet, and while he tried to steady himself against a table, the bartender took hold of his coat and shoved him through the swinging doors into the street, and advised him to make a quick getaway unless he wished to be arrested for attempting to murder a "poor and harmless working man".

For a week his conductor did not see Joe, who was, during every moment of this time, ceaselessly combing the slums, the dives, the police courts and even the "jungles" upon the outskirts of the city in a vain effort to get a glimpse of Kansas Shorty.

To some of the fellows whom he recognized as having been members of the "mob" which prevented his choking Kansas Shorty into a confession, he told the story of his missing brother and repeated the strange conversation that had passed between them before he felled the scoundrel to the pavement. These plingers, knitted together by the common knowledge that of all human vultures they are the most despised, had only shrugs for the unfortunate man, and when one of them, tiring of his repeated pleadings, condescended to hand him a mite of con-solation, all the information he cared to impart was contained in the rejoinder that "Kansas Shorty had jumped the city."

CHAPTER XIV.

"The Noble Work of the Salvation Army."

A most decided change had come over Joseph McDonald when he again reported himself ready for duty. Since his struggle with Kansas Shorty he had repeatedly weighed every word this rascal had spoken and adduced from it that something most dishonorable must have been Jim's fate, and the oftener he attempted to unravel the mystery that lay concealed behind the ill-omened remarks made by this scoundrel, the more morose he became from the constant strain, for his troubled conscience caused him to feel that he was equally to be blamed for any disgrace that might have overtaken his missing brother.

The more he worried the more he became resolved that even should he never be able to see his brother again, the chances that he would some day run across Kansas Shorty were far more favorable, as he well knew how drifters of his class roved aimlessly over the country as their fancy, the wanderlust, and more often the police drove them onward.

To find Kansas Shorty became an obsession with Joe. If luck favored him in his search, he planned to plead with the scoundrel, but should this prove of no avail, then he intended to strangle him until he would divulge the secret which shrouded Jim's fate.

Oftentimes, especially when late in the night, after the passengers had gone to sleep upon the coach seats, and Joe thought himself unobserved, his fellow trainmen, to whom he had confided his life's story, watched Joe, to whom a troubled conscience refused peace, raise his hands before him and slowly close the fingers with such suggestive motions, that it caused the trainmen to shudder when they imagined the same fingers executing like motions while entwined about Kansas Shorty's throat.

Joe's second hobby was to study the hobo monickers written upon or carved into the railroad company's property. From the time his train left the Chicago Terminal until it pulled into the Union Station at Omaha, where Joe's "trip" ended, he employed every spare moment while they stopped at stations or water tanks, to carefully read every hobo sign that the drifters passing to and fro over the line had left behind them, ever hoping to discover a clue to Kansas Shorty's whereabouts by finding his name-de-rail with a date and an arrow beneath it pointing in the direction he was traveling.

Joe's third and favorite hobby was to hunt hoboes who dared to beat their way upon his train. He finely discriminated between the man in search of employment, the harmless tramp who had fallen a victim to the wanderlust, the sneaking rogue who "toted" a six-shooter for the special purpose of killing human beings, preferring railroad employees and hoboes, and the rascal who had trained other people's sons to beg a living for him, exactly as an Italian organ grinder would train a performing monkey or bear. Many were the railroad lanterns Joe had to replace for those he broke over the heads of the two latter classes of tramps, especially the last ones, who clung even more obstinately to their road kids than a tiger clings to his prey. The youngsters he had rescued, if he was not able to send them safely home, he would turn over to proper authorities, for well he knew that each one of these runaway boys had not only somewhere a broken-hearted mother waiting for his return, but that, if they were not stopped drifting to the abyss while still young, with the evil training that depraved tramps gave them, it would be merely a matter of time before they too would have learned to destroy and pilfer railroad property; rob box cars and stations, and thus repay with almost brutal ingratitude those who had permitted them to travel unmolested upon their trains.

The years rolled quickly by and although Joe had now been in the company's employ for almost fifteen years, he refused every offer of promotion, preferring his humble trainman's job, that, although he had years ago given up all hope of ever seeing his brother James again, gave him a chance to atone for his own blighted past by his self-appointed mission, that of trying to combat single-handed and unassisted the most vitally important and yet most revolting phase of the whole tramp problem. His endeavor in this line caused much ridicule among his fellow railroad men and those who had stopped to listen to tramps and especially to plingers, whom Joe's unselfish work had deprived of victims and who denounced him as a "Stool Pigeon", as a "Spotter" and whatever other venomous attribute their black souls could hurl at him, in an attempt to damage his well earned reputation as a benefactor to humanity, who in spite of many threats of bodily injury, by pointing to the seriousness of the road kid evil, proved to the world its intimate connection with the never lessening, nay, ever increasing, numbers of thieving and murdering vagrants.

At both ends of his "run", at Chicago, as well as at Omaha, Joe had a rest of twelve hours before he again had to report for duty. One evening, just after he arrived at Omaha, his attention was attracted by a band of the Salvation Army holding a public service on a street corner. Their leader was loudly extorting and pleading with the crowd listening to his service, for penitents to come forward and permit the band to pray for their salvation. He was a good orator, and to hear him the better, Joe pushed his way through the crowd until he stood at the curb.

Just at the moment when some of his audience commenced to titter at the poor success the appeal seemed to have, forcing his way through the crowd came a half drunken, shaggy bearded and poorly dressed man, who, when he reached the open center of the meeting, pleaded with the Salvation Army's leader to pray for him. Undaunted by the fellow's rough appearance and the very evident marks of his craving for strong drink, the leader shook his hand and after he bade him welcome asked him as a primary step towards complete salvation to make a public confession of his sins.

Sobered by the solemnity of the moment the penitent wretch straightened and then gave a brief review of his life. It was the oft-repeated story of a runaway boy, hailing from a good family, drifting into hobo-companionship with all the rum, filth and crime that such association implies, and ended by telling that on this day, after having so wantonly wasted the best years of his life, he had made up his mind to end it all by placing his head upon the rails. On his way to the railway yards he had stopped to listen to the service of the Salvation Army, and when he heard their leader plead for lost souls, especially those who had been rejected by every other denomination, he felt it to be an act of God that had caused him to stop, and he came forward to try and make a second and better start in life.

When he finished his pitiful story of a blasted life, there was hardly a dry eye amongst the listeners, and taking advantage of the good impression the confession had made, the Salvation Army leader asked all those who were believers in Christ to offer up a silent prayer for the penitent sinner.

Joe joined the many others who complied with this request, and holding his cap before him, he bent his head in prayer. Then a strange incident occurred, for just as he replaced his cap the same repentant wretch for whose regeneration he had just prayed, came towards him and while tears rolled down his seamed face he stretched forth his hands and pleaded, "James McDonald, unfathomable are the ways of the merciful God, for here at the moment when I had resolved to henceforth lead a clean life he has sent you so I could beg your pardon for the greatest wrong a human being could inflict upon a harmless boy, that is, to wantonly spoil his future. James McDonald, I recognized your white hair streak when you lowered your head to pray for the salvation of the very man whom you had far better reason to curse. Will you not now forgive me, whom you have known as Kansas Shorty, and who will seek in the morning the first honest job he has ever done in his whole life?" Joe, dumfounded at meeting the fellow whom, although aged and disfigured by the unnatural life he had been leading, he now recognized as the tramp for whom he had searched for so many years, held his peace, for he recalled how he had at Chicago spoiled by undue haste his chance to discover the fate of his missing brother, who had resembled him so much that Kansas Shorty for a second time made the same error in their identity.

He told the wretch that he forgave him, and then drew back and became lost in the crowd, but while he stood well out of Kansas Shorty's view, he never took his eyes off the form of the new recruit of that immense army of human wrecks which the Salvationists have dragged out of saloons, gutters, penal institutions and back from suicide to convert and transform them into useful members of society.

A Drunken, Shaggy Bearded and Poorly Dressed Man Pushed Himself Through the Crowd, Which Listened to the Salvation Army's Leader Plea for Penitents to Come forward.

When the Salvation Army's street service had been concluded, led by flying flags and keeping step to the beating of a drum they marched to their prayer hall. Kansas Shorty, supported in his unsteady gait by two brethren of the Army, walked in the midst of the procession, while Joe kept some distance in the rear, never permitting his eyes to stray off the shambling form of the man who held the key to the riddle that had so effectively spoiled Joe's joy of life.

After the army had entered the meeting hall, Joe called on the leader and gave him a brief outline of his past and asked him to assist him to cause Kansas Shorty to make a complete confession. The leader called his latest convert into his private office and explained to him that it was not James but his twin brother Joe of whom he had begged forgiveness, and he spoke so earnestly to the penitent outcast that the latter made a clean breast of all he knew concerning James McDonald, and although the leader as well as Joe tried to make him reveal more, he steadfastly maintained that after Jim's arrest at Denver he had left that city in a hurry and did not know anything further concerning his fate.

When Joe left the Salvation Army's headquarters it was he who had to seek support to keep himself from falling, as the information he had just received unnerved him so completely that he could barely walk, for what Kansas Shorty had told not only proved that with Jim's disappearance he had lost every member of his family, but that his brother had also disgraced their good name.

Late that night while he rolled restlessly about upon his bed, tormented by this last disappointment, and while he puzzled his feverish mind, a strong resentment came over him that Jim should have permitted himself to be so easily led astray by a good-for-nothing tramp, but when he remembered the circumstances of his own experience with Slippery, the yegg, brotherly love got the mastery over him and an idea flashed through his mind, that if Jim had been arrested at Denver the court records there should show the sentence the Judge had imposed, and that, although it seemed merely a forlorn hope, there was a chance to pick up the trail that would lead to something, and even if he failed to accomplish anything, for the sake of his own satisfaction, that he had done everything possible to clear up his brother's disappearance, he decided to leave on the morning for Denver.

CHAPTER XV.
"Forgive and Forget."

In the morning Joe put his plan into execution by applying for and receiving a month's leave of absence, and taking the first train, he arrived early on the second day at Denver. Here he hastened to the court house and had the city clerk search in musty records and when he came close to the date that Joe had calculated tallied with Kansas Shorty's story, they found James McDonald's name, and the sentence the judge had imposed which read: "Imprisonment in the Colorado State Reformatory at Buena Vista until of age."

This second step towards unravelling his missing brother's fate pleased Joe so well that before another hour had rolled around he was aboard a train bound for Buena Vista to continue the search there. At day break he arrived at this pretty mountain city and hired a livery rig and drove to the reformatory, situated upon the outskirts of Buena Vista. Here he called at the warden's office, and after stating his errand, again old records were searched, which showed that James Mc-Donald had been received at the institution, but on account of exemplary behavior had soon after his arrival been paroled into the care of a rancher named Holmes. Then the warden recalled the case and explained to him that Jim not only had become Mr. Holmes' son-in-law by marrying his daughter, but that he was the proud father of a son and a daughter and was considered a respected member of the community. He also advised Joe to drive to Mr. Holmes' ranch, as it was only about ten miles down the valley.

It was almost dinner time when Joe arrived at Mr. Holmes' handsome home, and when he saw a man standing at the gate as he approached, he immediately knew that it was his long lost brother, as he still resembled Joe, as much as in the past.

"Jim," cried Joe, as he swung himself from the buggy, and "Brother Joe," came back the prompt reply, and then with tears of joy streaming from their eyes they embraced each other, and after their affectionate greeting they repaired to a nearby bench, and while holding his at-last-found brother's hands Joe remarked, not aware that his brother did not know that their mother and their eldest brother Donald had disappeared in Canada, a land almost as large as the United States: "Brother Jim, there is just one thing in this world that would add to our happiness and that is, I wish our mother were here to join us at this happy reunion," but hardly had he finished when Jim replied: "Joe, now that we have at last found each other, let us do what for so many years I have promised my wife and babies, should the good Lord answer my prayers and permit me to meet you again, and travel to Rugby and surprise our mother and plead for her forgiveness before she has passed from among the mortals, as she has no doubt suffered untold anguish in all the weary years since we ran away, as I have not dared during all this time to visit her nor write to her until I was assured that you were still among the living."

'Jim', Cried Joe, As He Swung Himself from the Buggy, and 'Brother Joe'
Came Back the Prompt Reply, and then With Tears of Joy Streaming Down
their Faces the Reunited Brothers Embraced Each Other.

Joe merely nodded his head as if assenting, as he did not wish to spoil his brother's gladness at this moment by telling of the fateful letter across the face of which was written: "Moved to Canada. Present address unknown," nor of the many official letters he had in his trunk from the Governor of every Canadian Province and many other officials, all of whom had searched in vain for their missing mother, and, too, he recalled those long hours of fearful remorse behind the locked door of his room, and decided to withhold this knowledge from his brother as well he realized that it would cause heart wounds which would require years to heal.

Joe now gave his brother a brief review of his own career since they were separated, and finished by telling him that his present occupation was that of a railroad employee.

At this moment an elderly gentleman approached and Joe introduced him to his brother as Mr. Holmes, his father-in-law, who, while Jim left to arrange for Joe's dinner, told Joe that after he had engaged Jim, the latter had proven himself so reliable that when a few years later his only daughter, Dorothy, who had been sent east to finish her education, returned and had fallen head over heels in love with Jim, he not only gave his paternal blessing, but on their marriage day gave her for a wedding present a deed to the ranch.

Just then the dinner bell rang, and when they came to the house Mrs. James McDonald with her son, a lad of eight, and her daughter, a pretty girl of five, were waiting for them, and after Jim had introduced Joe he called his attention to the fact that his baby girl was named after her Aunt Helen who disappeared so mysteriously, and that the children had the McDonald family mark, the streak of white hair upon their heads.

After dinner Jim called Joe into his private office and pleaded with him to forsake the railroad and make his future home upon the ranch. But it was quite a while before Joe would even listen to his proposition, but when Jim assured his brother that he could not think of having to part with him again he finally consented to the change.

During the remainder of the afternoon Joe was busy writing his resignation and arranging to have his property transferred from Chicago, while Mr. Holmes and Jim were away from the house overseeing the work of the ranch. After Joe had finished his correspondence he took a seat in a rocking chair upon the porch from where he had a grand view of the fertile valley of the Arkansas and the snow capped mountain ranges beyond.

A little later his sister-in-law joined him, and although she sat in another rocker close to Joe's, he found it impossible to engage her in a conversation, try as he might, as she persisted in staring him in the face. Chagrined at what he thought to be an affront, he suddenly blurted out: "Mrs. McDonald, is there something about my face that interests you?" Instead of an answer the lady who had turned a ghastly pallor handed him a small, paper wrapped parcel. Joe opened the same, and then after he hastily scanned its contents he speechlessly stared at his hostess. "Great God in Heaven," exclaimed Joe, breaking the suspense and unable to better express his amazement at the singular turn affairs had taken, while with a trembling hand he drew forth from the paper a small leather purse. "Can it be possible that you, Mrs. McDonald, are 'Babe', the girl I met fifteen years ago in Chicago, and whose timely assistance gave me a start upon the narrow path?" "I am the same girl, Joe," she quietly replied, "and it was for the express purpose of getting a chance to tell you that I am 'Babe' that I stared so rudely into your face, because I knew that now or never had come the climax in the lives of those who had in former days known each other as 'Babe' and 'Dakota Joe'." Then she took the small leather purse out of Joe's trembling hand and again wrapped it in the paper, and after striking a match that she had brought for this purpose, she held the lighted splinter against the paper, and when the hungry flames leaped up she threw the burning parcel upon the lawn below, and while they both watched the fire consume the fateful purse, Mrs. McDonald took Joe's hand into her own and while they pressed a mute, but none the less oath-bound promise to each other, she solemnly said: "For the sake of Jim's happy home and our innocent children, for the sake of the name all of us bear, and the many years I have lived an honorable life to atone for what occurred before the day when I last saw you in Chicago, I plead with you, whom, to my horror, I later discovered to be my own husband's missing brother, to let the past be forgiven, to be buried in silence and be forever hereafter forgotten."

CHAPTER XVI.
"All is Well, that Ends Well."

Joe's sojourn at his brother's home had reached the fifth year, and although he outwardly gave every indication of being perfectly satisfied, his visit had actually been a continued torture to him, for his brother became from day to day more insistent to pay their mother at Rugby the long intended visit. Joe, who had never yet dared to acquaint his brother with the truth concerning her disappearance, found it the hardest task of his life to dissuade Jim from making the journey and to find plausible excuses to prevent him from sending a letter to Rugby.

The "skeleton in the closet" rattled ever more threateningly. "Next Spring," was Jim's ultimate reply, while his fist came angrily down upon the parlor table, after he and Joe had another of their evermore heated arguments as to the why and why not they should visit their mother, "Dorothy and the children and I will certainly visit Rugby, and if you do not care to join us to see her, we shall go without you," and then he arose and left the room.

Singular indeed are the ways of Providence, for with the arrival of Spring a Canadian colonization agent found his way into the fertile valley of the Arkansas, where every acre of land was pre-empted and worth a huge price. Backed by an unlimited number of well written pamphlets which he freely distributed, he described Canada as equal to the land of Canaan; that homesteads were begging there for settlers and that land would bountifully produce anything, considering the northern latitude.

Jim, who had saved a large portion of the annual income the ranch had earned became greatly interested in that part of the colonizer's story, in which he spoke of the enormous dividends that investments would bring, and when the agent explained to him that at a small additional outlay he could combine a Canadian trip with his journey to Rugby, this settled the matter.

There was not a single loop hole left for Joe to prevent the journey, and when Jim and his wife commenced to pack their trunks, ready to leave for Canada on the coming morning, with or without Joe, the latter with a heavy heart followed suit, intending to ease as much as possible his brother's grief when Jim discovered that his journey to Rugby had been made in vain.

In the morning Mr. Holmes drove Joe, Jim and his wife and children to the railroad station, but when the brothers asked at the ticket window for a round trip ticket to Canada, via Rugby, they were informed—to the dismay of Jim and to the joy of Joe, as this spelled additional delay—that the ticket would be only good for stop-overs upon their return journey.

Soon they were aboard their train, and while Jim and his family had the time of their lives, Joe could hardly conceal the dread which racked his conscience when he thought how pitifully different would be their homeward trip.

The outward journey ended at Edmonton, the hustling "Gate City to the Arctic", and then they commenced their return trip, stopping at Saskatoon, the beautiful "Hub City of the Saskatchewan"; at Regina, that stately "Queen City of the North West;" at Calgary, the "Gem City of the Rockies", and travelled from the latter to Winnipeg, the "Chicago of Canada."

They intended that Winnipeg should be their last stop, as from there they meant to return via Rugby to their Colorado ranch.

While viewing the sights of cosmopolitan Winnipeg with its wide streets and beautiful avenues, their progress was stopped in front of the City Hall by policemen, who held back a curious crowd, while they were unloading several patrol wagons filled with oddly dressed foreigners. Joe pushed himself close to one of the policemen and inquired the reason of their arrest, and the obliging guardian of the peace explained to him that they were "Doukhobors", a religious sect that on account of persecution had left Russia, and although they made first-class settlers, some of them had been arrested on account of queer practices which conflicted with the laws of Canada, and which, despite repeated warnings, they refused to discontinue.

By this time the prisoners had been transferred into the city hall, and the officer volunteered to see to it that Joe and his friends would find a good vantage point from where they could watch a Canadian court trial. Joe accepted the officer's kind offer, and the latter opened a path through the densely crowded court room for the McDonalds, who were soon standing at the railing that separated the prisoners from the public.

Amongst the more than a score of prisoners were several women, all of whom were old hags with the exception of one, who was really good looking considering that she wore the same homely, gray homespun dress and black shawl that did service for headwear, worn by all the women of her sect.

All noise subsided when the judge entered the court room. He was a stern-faced gentleman, and wore a white wig and a black robe, which, although they gave him the appearance of a patriarch, also added greatly to the austerity of his exalted office.

It was against the tenets of the Doukhobors to employ legal counsel to defend them, and so the trial was quickly finished. The young woman was the only one amongst them who could understand the English language, and she answered the judge's questions, and when the sentence had been passed, the others in their anxiety to hear from her how long a term they had been condemned to, almost mobbed her, and in the struggle the black shawl covering her head fell to the floor.

"Look, Jim, look!" shouted Joe to his brother above the din the Doukhobors made, while at the same time he pointed towards the young woman's head, upon which one braid of white hair stood plainly out against a black braid on each side of it. "She is the first human being I ever saw or heard of that had the birthmark of the McDonald's." Then a vague suspicion flashed through his mind and he asked the officer to bring the woman over to where he was standing so he could question her concerning her past.

While the judge and the barristers were engaged in writing the commitment papers, Joe asked the woman to tell him who was her mother, and when she pointed at a wrinkled hag, he had the policeman stand the latter beside her daughter, who now acted as interpreter. Now Joe had Jim's daughter stand beside the younger woman, and when the old hag noted the resemblance between the two she paled and commenced to weep. Aided by the policeman, and the promise that if the Doukhobor woman told the truth concerning the young woman's parentage she would not be molested, and greatly influenced by the fact that her sect, like the Quakers, consider telling an untruth a mortal sin, she told the following story:

While she and her husband in company with many others of their sect were crossing the Atlantic, during the stormy winter voyage, her only child, a little girl, died and was buried at sea. They landed in America and were loaded aboard an immigrant train, which several days later stopped in a snow covered prairie. Looking out of the coach window, the bereaved mother saw a little tot, just the size of their own "Maritzka", playing in the snow below the window, and yearning for her departed baby she had climbed from the train and petted the little child, who instead of being frightened by the strange woman, permitted her to kiss its rosy cheeks, and while she felt the tot's chubby hands and soft limbs, the mother love which she used to lavish upon her own Maritzka got the upper hand of her, and noting that no one was guarding this smiling baby girl, and that no homes were near, she could not resist the temptation to have this child replace the one God had taken from her. Realizing that the child's clothing did not match her own, she quickly undressed the tot, and after she had wrapped it in her shawl she climbed aboard the train, which at this moment commenced to pull away. While she dressed the child in the clothes which had belonged to her own child, she discovered that she had overlooked a locket that hung around its neck, and that ever since that day had kept this place. She now caused her kidnapped daughter to take off and hand this locket to Joe, and when he opened it he found his late father's and his mother's picture in it, and an inscription that read, "Henry McDonald to Ethel, his wife."

Then Joe and Jim quickly proved to the young woman that they were truly her brothers, and promised her that they would properly look after her every need if she would part with the foreign woman, who, in her ignorance, had not only spoiled her life, but had caused her father's death. She consented to go with them and took a tearful farewell of the Doukhobor woman, who had been a mother to her all these years, and although poor herself, had provided her with a fair education.

The story of the strange finding of their long lost sister traveled through the court room, and when it came to the attention of the judge, he suspended the young woman's sentence so her brothers could take her back with them to the States. He was anxious to hear from their own lips the story of the strange recovery, and he induced Joe to repeat to him every fact connected with the loss and the finding of their sister. After Joe had finished, the judge seemed so well pleased with the story he told, that he begged them to be seated so he could send for a reporter of Winnipeg's leading paper, "The Manitoba Free Press", so all the world could read of the wonderful recovery of their sister. They gladly consented, and then the judge gave whispered instructions to a messenger.

When the messenger returned the judge arose from his chair and met him half way across the court room, and both entered an adjacent jury chamber, from which the judge a few minutes later emerged and beckoned to the McDonalds to join him in this room. When they entered the jury chamber they found themselves in the presence of an elderly lady seated at a table, whose silvery hair lent an added charm to the sad expression of her face, and whom the judge introduced as the reporter sent by the "Free Press" to write their interesting story for that paper.

Joe then repeated the story of the mysterious disappearance of their baby sister, and while he narrated her recovery after so many years, his strange tale caused the attentively listening lady reporter to exclaim: "How wonderful are the ways of our Lord." When Joe had finished the judge inquired of the brothers what their intentions were concerning their sister's future, to which question Jim answered that they would take the earliest train to Rugby and that he thought it would be best to leave her there in care of their mother and their eldest brother Donald.

While he was talking the judge had taken off his wig and laid aside his robe. Hardly had Jim finished unfolding his plan, than the judge wheeled around, and when the brothers looked in the direction of his uplifted finger, which was pointing towards the back of his head, to their complete amazement they saw there the same strange streak of snow white hair that distinguished every member of the McDonald family. Ere they could utter a single syllable the judge again faced them and told them that he himself, was their brother Donald McDonald, and that after they ran away from home he and their mother had emigrated to Canada, where by hard work and frugality they had managed to send him to a university, from which, after he had studied law, he had gradually been promoted to a judgeship.

Joe, whose conscience had troubled him ever since the fatal moment when his unopened letter had been returned to him from Rugby, broke the profound silence that prevailed in the room after the judge's revelation as to his identity, by asking the one question ever supreme in his mind. He wished to know if his newly found brother Donald could not tell them their mother's present address, so he and Jim could hasten to her and beg her pardon for all the trouble their running away from their home must have caused her.

Tears were welling into the judge's eyes when he pointed to the lady at the table, and then with his voice choking with emotion he said: "This lady is not a reporter, but is our own dear mother, and I am sure that she will gladly forgive you for your thoughtless boyish prank, for you plainly show how grieved and repentant you are, and how anxious you will henceforth be to atone by true filial devotion in the future for the nameless woe you have brought upon her life in the past."

As if spurred on by a common impulse, Joe and Jim humbly knelt before the sweet faced lady in whose careworn face they readily recognized the countenance of their own once so happy mother, and pleaded for her forgiveness. While they were still waiting for the words which would end a penance stretching over twenty weary years, she arose from her chair, and trembling with emotion lifted her withered arms high above her head, and with a face that bespoke the joy which had at last blessed her life, she pronounced this benediction:

"Oh, Henry McDonald, my dear departed husband, how I wish that at this happy moment you were standing beside me to assist me in blessing those who have come home, and praising the good Lord above us from now until my children bury me, for having this day, after so many sorrowful years, mercifully answered my tearful prayers."

This maternal blessing was followed by a most affectionate greeting and then the happy family repaired to Judge Donald McDonald's stately mansion where they further celebrated their reunion.

When some weeks later Joe and Jim and the latter's family returned to the Buena Vista ranch they not only had their sister Helen accompany them, but had persuaded their beloved mother to take a pleasure trip to their Colorado home, and according to the latest reports the judge is having the time of his life trying to induce the happy mother to return to her home in Canada.

This was Canada Joe's story.